GAY
UNIONS

GAY UNIONS

In the Light of Scripture, Tradition, and Reason

GRAY TEMPLE

CHURCH PUBLISHING
New York

The quotation on p. 171 is from *A Sleep of Prisoners* by Christopher Fry, copyright 1951 by Christopher Fry. Used by permission of Oxford University Press, Inc.

Cataloging-in-Publication Data is available from the Library of Congress

ISBN 0-89869-457-4

Church Publishing Incorporated
445 Fifth Avenue
New York, NY 10016
www.churchpublishing.org

5 4 3 2 1

Contents

Foreword		7
Preface		13
ONE	"Can We Talk?"	17
TWO	Scripture	35
THREE	Tradition	101
FOUR	Reason	121
Epilogue		171

Foreword

To have lived in the twentieth and early twenty-first centuries is to have experienced some of the most extraordinary and rapid cultural transformations ever to have taken place in human history. Many things taken for granted by our grandparents and great-grandparents about the hierarchical relation of the races or the immutable roles of men and women now seem almost unimaginable. Patterns of large-scale immigration currently challenge the assumption of ethnic, linguistic, and religious homogeneity as the necessary basis of the nation-state. Medical technologies raise questions about the beginning and end of life that earlier generations literally could not imagine. The list of such transformations could easily be extended.

These are not merely social changes, though they are certainly that. Nor are they simply institutional changes, though each has profound implications for governmental, ecclesial, and other institutions. More fundamentally, these are transformations of the very ways we think about the world and ourselves. In every case, as people grapple with changed circumstances and new claims, the concepts they have taken for granted no longer seem unproblematic. This is not a comfortable experience. Human beings desire to live in a world that is intelligible and reliably known: what's what, who's who, and how it all fits together. To be sure, we recognize that, historically speaking, our mental furniture has been rearranged fairly often. But it is still disconcerting to go through the process. A scene from the science fiction spoof *Men in Black* represents it well. Just after "Agent J" (Will Smith) has had his first encounter with a space alien, the more experienced "Agent K" (Tommy Lee Jones) explains to him: "Fifteen hundred years ago everybody *knew* the earth was the center of the universe; five hundred years ago, everybody *knew* the earth was flat; and fifteen minutes ago you *knew* that people were alone on this planet. Imagine what you'll *know* tomorrow."

Among the seismic upheavals of recent decades has been a profound challenge to traditional ways of thinking about human sexuality. The claims of homosexual persons that their sexual orientation be understood not as deviant or pathological, but as a natural and normal form of human sexuality is transforming what we *knew* about sexuality. Moreover, significant transformations of understanding about one thing always have implications for other areas of concern. How do new conceptions of human sexuality affect the way we think about marriage and family? It is not difficult to see why these matters would engender passionate debate. For our culture, sexuality is one of the core features of identity; marriage and family, one of its fundamental institutions.

Grappling with radical transformations of understanding poses particular challenges for Christians. We understand ourselves and our world through the saving work of God, not only as we experience it in our own lives but also as we encounter it in Holy Scripture and in the traditions of the church. Thus the moral urgencies that arise from new ways of understanding have to be examined in light of biblical witness and the theological heritage of the church. This is no simple matter. For one thing, the issues we wish to raise simply may not be the ones addressed directly by scripture. Even when they

8

appear to be, we often come up against the realization that the conceptual and social systems of the biblical world are often sharply different from those of modernity. Discerning the underlying theological truths that both make sense of the biblical witness and provide guidance for our own situation requires insight, honesty, and a deep trust in God. It isn't easy, but it can be done.

In *Gay Unions: In the Light of Scripture, Tradition, and Reason* Gray Temple attempts to do just that. Part of what gives this book its passion and its moral authority is that Temple is someone who has changed his mind about the issue of sacramental equality for gays and lesbians. He has thought "from the inside" on both sides of the question. And in order to explain his transformed convictions to his erstwhile conservative colleagues and to the rest of the church, he has done his biblical and theological homework with a thoroughness that few have undertaken. What he has found and shares with others in this book is that "a respectful reading of the Bible allows and may in fact require a good-faith case to be made for the sacramental equality of homosexual Christians."

Temple's book makes several important contributions to the discussion. One is its demonstration that the assumption that all people in all times and places have thought about sex and sexuality in more or less the same way that we do is just not so. Uncovering how the ancients thought about these matters can be an eye-opener, but the issue is of great importance. If we do not understand their assumptions about sex and sexuality, then we cannot adequately interpret the biblical texts that are often at the center of controversy in discussions of sacramental equality for homosexual persons.

Another contribution the book makes is its careful consideration of the biblical passages most often cited by conservatives and liberals alike. Too often, people think they already know what the Bible says about homosexuality, having heard a few verses taken out of context and brandished as conversation stoppers. Temple insists that we actually read the texts — closely, and with attention to their context. The result is a much more nuanced and often surprising understanding of what the Bible actually says. Through his careful reading of the biblical texts, Temple shows that supporters of sacramental equality need not shy away from the Bible "as though fearing what we'd find in its pages." Rather, he boldly reclaims the Bible as the essential common ground upon which conversation about sacramental equality must take place.

The chapter on reason makes a different kind of contribution. Although it does take up and refute arguments against sacramental equality of gays and lesbians, in this chapter Temple expands the notion of what reason encompasses to include an account of the experiences with God and others that led him to understand differently. As he observes, people do not usually change their minds in response to arguments; change comes from direct personal experience. "We only change our minds after our hearts change." Reading his account reminds one that this debate about sacramental equality is not about abstractions but persons. It also explains how he came to be one of the most passionate and eloquent defenders of sacramental equality.

In other hands a book entitled *Gay Unions: In the Light of Scripture, Tradition, and Reason* might be both difficult and dull. To be sure, Temple asks a lot of his readers, but he is never dull. To read this book is to set off on a journey with a guide who is witty, passionate, outspoken, and relentlessly honest. Conservative and liberal readers will both wince at all-too-accurate observations of how they come across to one another. But both sets of readers will learn much and be challenged to think more deeply.

Carol A. Newsom
Professor of Old Testament/Hebrew Bible
Candler School of Theology
Emory University

Preface

Any discussion of what we call "homosexuality" will be passionate.

It must embrace the passions that drive our lesbigay friends to risk all and seek and love their partners in the face of social pressures that can mount to murderousness. It must take part in the passion that allows these sisters and brothers to embrace their creation, their Creator, and themselves as creatures of a God who "...don't create no junk."

It must embrace the passions of men and women whose opposition to the "homosexual agenda" is energized by fears and loathings secreted in their souls' darkest chambers. Less passionate but equally opposed are those who honestly believe that affirming homosexual persons will corrupt their nation, their parishes, their families, their marriages. On my heart are former leaders in my congregation who felt called away when our views on the sacramental status of gay and lesbian believers began to diverge. Included also are friends and colleagues in the Charismatic Renewal for whom my change of heart and mind betokened apostatic defection. And the Cycle of Prayer reminds me of a host of Anglicans overseas (in many cases my literal hosts) for whom these matters warrant schism.

I am neither homosexual nor an opponent of "homosexuals." So what passion do I bring to this discussion? When I strive to appear dispassionate, what strong feelings am I trying to govern?

I bring first a lifelong passion for Jesus, whose personal presence erases any need to distinguish between "them and us" for any purpose whatever.

I bring a lifelong love for the Episcopal Church. Listening to the shibboleths and buzz words that characterize public Christianity today, I thank God repeatedly for our church. Without her courageous witness and eminently sensible stances — and without her willing embrace of people of all sorts — I would continue to adore Jesus Christ. But I would no longer risk calling myself a Christian for fear of being thought a bigot.

I bring a passion for my wife, Jean, without whose love and devotion I could never have grown up and who taught me the nutritive power of intimacy.

I bring a passionate love and pain for erstwhile friends who could no longer afford our friendship once God changed my mind on these issues.

I bring a passionate love and admiration for lesbian and gay friends whom I eventually discovered I was no longer willing to betray. Chuck used to come witness to me, demonstrating an integrity I finally had to believe. Louie modeled (and models) the truth with charm and humility. Bruce persistently practices courage and endurance in the face of pressures I tremble to imagine. Rick chose to conclude his life in my strife-torn parish, forgiving those who openly despised him as he died. Charlene offered me soul-penetrating friendship as she died and bequeathed to Jean and me the love of Elizabeth — and, by eventual extension, Lou Ellen. The faces of the members of the Host Committee in the Diocese of Atlanta, gay and straight, are always before me when fear tempts me to backpedal.

I bring a passionate admiration for "straight" Christians who have publicly stood alongside gay and lesbian fellow Christians.

Jane, a conservative Charismatic, told me on her way out of church, "I was praying about all this last night and the Lord told me he loves these people and that I have to change my mind." Bennett openly disavowed a position he had previously espoused as bishop, forfeiting the approval of a wide public.

In the pages that follow, God grant me the grace to betray none of them — on any side.

ONE

"Can We Talk?"

Now is the time for your loving, Dear,
And a time for your company,
Now when the light of reason fails
And fires burn on the sea,
Now in this Age of Confusion I
Have need for your company.

— RICHARD FARINA

"Can we talk?"

Most of us don't like hearing that question. We're not sure if it's an inquiry, the introduction to criticism, or the prelude to an ultimatum. It often signals a return to a topic we started finding tedious some time back.

Something like that is going on in the Episcopal Church. Some of us want to "talk" more than others. For more than thirty years members of the Episcopal Church have been poking at the question, "Can we talk?" — about the sacramental equality or inequality of our gay and lesbian fellow worshipers.

What do I mean by sacramental equality/inequality? I mean that, like the rest of us, gay and lesbian church members are entitled to Baptism, the Eucharist, Confirmation, Penance, and Unction. And they get stewardship visits each fall. But their access to Ordination has been restricted to the celibate until quite recently — and the church as a whole has not officially changed her mind about that access yet. The church still officially, if no longer uniformly, restricts gay members from Holy Matrimony. So long as homosexual members are not equally entitled to seek the latter two sacraments they are not sacramentally equal to the rest of the church.

The matter of the sacramental status of homosexual church members has been on the church's table since the Sixty-Fifth General Convention in 1973. Though that convention reiterated the church's teaching on sex (sex is only godly between married people) and went on to wield it as a prohibition specifically against homosexual Christians (because homosexual couplings do not occur within marriage, they cannot be seen as godly), the convention nevertheless recognized a "discontinuity" between this teaching and the experience of some of the church's homosexual members. That convention launched the first of many appeals for discussion of these topics.

In my observation it's mostly liberals who have responded to the request for dialogue and conservatives who are less willing. The conversations I've been a part of typically have been launched with a set of rules, sometimes with actual training exercises in exploratory listening, all designed to assure a fair hearing for differing opinions. Those rules derive from studies of group dynamics and conflict management that are of more interest to liberals than to conservatives, judging from the people you normally see at such training sessions.

Has any fruit at all emerged out of those three decades of talk? It's difficult to tell. I cannot presently recall one person who has reported a change of mind as a result of such discussions, though you'd expect they would have some effect. Psychologists tell us that when people argue, a "drift toward the middle" tends to occur, as though the very process of allowing your meanings to move through my neural circuitry leaves some of my switches permanently on. That drift can expand my thinking even if I'm not aware of changing my mind. Perhaps the drift to the middle accounts for the General Convention's recent decision to allow the election and subsequent consecration of a gay priest living openly "married" to another man. The majority of deputies and bishops assembled in 2003 were better able at least to imagine such a thing than their predecessors had been in 1973.

Certainly secular culture has moved in a more permissive direction in recent years. Several European countries currently offer marriage to same-sex couples, as do parts of Canada. Many others offer civil unions with the legal standing of marriage. In our country, Hawaii's Supreme Court first flirted with the notion; New Jersey instituted domestic partnerships; Vermont recognized civil unions as tantamount to marriage; and the Massachusetts Supreme Court recently took the whole plunge. The mayors of several towns — beginning spectacularly with San Francisco — began issuing marriage licenses to same-sex couples. Yet the sentiment in favor of sacramental equality in the Episcopal Church is anything but uniform — and the opposition is stiffer, better organized, more precisely networked, and better funded than previously. So I think we must conclude that our talk so far has not gone fully to anyone's satisfaction.

I AM WRITING this book to friends. I treasure friendships on both sides of the debate — and among the complacent middle 60 percent. I have been in enough conversations with friends all over the spectrum to know that no one's mind is going to change as a result of reading my thoughts in favor of sacramental equality. But I have stood on both sides of the divide somewhat publicly and have loved and respected the people I stood with. I know from personal acquaintance that we can all do a better job of talking than we've managed so far.

To begin with, what do friends call each other? Let's use the label "liberals" on the 20 percent of us who favor Bishop Gene Robinson's episcopate and are hopeful for the thaw into sacramental equality for gays and lesbians that it may betoken. Historians remind us that a century ago the word "liberal" (applied to theology) meant things most of us would neither recognize nor espouse. Still we can use that label as a convenience, however cautiously. And the 20 percent who energetically regret that action and don't welcome its implications? Let's call them what most call themselves: "conservatives," many of whom are Evangelicals.

Now nobody likes labels — and nobody likes being labeled. As the girl in the bar ironically quipped to Woody Allen, "Oh, I don't mind being reduced to a cultural stereotype." But of course she did. Still labels save time if we use them to launch or pursue a conversation rather than to close one. These labels are shorthand and in no way betoken disrespect or reductionism — at least not from my fountain pen. "Liberal" and "conservative" are somewhat more descriptive than, say, "shirts" and "skins."

I wish this little book would change people's minds, but I doubt it will. So short of that I'd like it to have some impact on the way we talk among ourselves on each side of the ditch — and the way we holler across it. It's possible that some of these suggestions may be of service to friends who oppose the Robinson decision.

I also want to alert both sides to a truth that gets routinely disregarded: those who favor the Robinson decision have substantive biblical, traditional, and reasoned warrant to do so. It does not enhance the accuracy of thinking on either side of the aisle to describe one party as the biblical or orthodox party and other as worldly or trendy or revisionist. In discussions I carry on with conservative friends, that reality almost never gets acknowledged; nor do I find traces of it in conservative writings and documents. What is more surprising and troubling is how often friends on the liberal side of the aisle are unaware of the biblical, traditional, and reasoned substantiation for their humanistic sensibilities. When liberals get tempted to abandon rigorous attention to the three-stranded cord of Anglican authority — most especially the biblical strand — the conservative indictment becomes a self-fulfilling prophecy. I'd like for this book to correct that — on both sides.

I am pleading this not only to reinforce the liberal position with biblical and traditional proof-texts. Liberals must go beyond the surface of the argument. They must acknowledge that conservatives and Evangelicals love the Bible deeply and sincerely. Many also embrace with gratitude to God what they understand as Christian traditions. If liberals oppose conservatives on the matter of sacramental equality for gay and lesbian believers — as in justice we must — while refusing to demonstrate rigorously the biblical and traditional underpinnings for our stance, we estrange our conservative siblings from their own scripture and tradition by inadvertently maneuvering them to clutch defensively only restricted portions of it — the portions that appear to them to sustain their current beliefs. Liberals would do well to respect conservatives enough to trust that the latter love the Bible itself more than they love their own opinions. We serve them when we offer something solid to push against — as indeed they serve us. Glibly replying to a "biblical" argument with something like, "The Law of Love supersedes the Love of Law" sounds cute. But it's not a response; it's a disengagement.

Our talk would be enriched if liberals did not struggle with an undeclared guilty conscience about having ceded the Bible and Christian tradition to the Evangelicals. Some of us indeed have abandoned those treasures, assuming that they were inimical to justice. But in so doing, we left our own money on the table. In a recent (cordial) exchange of e-mails, Professor Robert Gagnon complained to me about an Episcopal liberal's comparison of the Levitical prohibitions against male-male coitus with the prohibitions against eating shellfish; such glibness trivialized the discussion in his opinion. I sought to excuse the comment (from a bright man who is also a personal friend) as the sort of remark that high-velocity interviews provoke. But I conceded that at least some make such glib comments in the absence of any serious engagement with the Bible on this question.

We liberals tend to be somewhat chary of the Bible and of church tradition. Some of us are refugees from religious backgrounds in which scripture and/or tradition were instruments of oppression. All of us liberal clergy shelter people in our congregations who're trying to recover from religious abuse. Yet in the process of becoming refuges that embody a Christ-like humanism, we have as a party tended, I think, to move the discussion away from the Bible as though fearing what we'd find in its pages.

That was brought home to me forcibly in August and September 2003 following the General Convention in Minneapolis. I had a flurry of phone calls and e-mails from fellow clergy who were under bombardment from aggrieved parishioners.

They knew that my parish and I had undergone such an upheaval a decade ago during an adult Sunday school investigation of these matters that had turned explosive. Indeed when I, as an openly avowed "Charismatic," announced that God had changed my mind about the sacramental equality of gay people, the next few years became what the Chinese call "interesting times." But that imbroglio had made me do my Bible homework finally. Both the Bible itself and my new convictions survived the homework handily. I was now hearing from friends who were doing their own homework and wanting some collaboration. (Once you're graduated and ordained, that's no longer considered cheating.) They knew in their hearts and in their prayers that the Gene Robinson decision was impelled by the Holy Spirit — but how to display its congruence with the church's Bible and tradition? I originally drafted the contents of the following chapter as an offering to my colleagues. My hope in spreading it further is that liberals reassert our claim to the Holy Bible and do so in a rigorous manner. Surely Evangelicals would benefit from such an engagement.

So this is an attempt to demonstrate — in the most readable form someone like me can produce — that the liberal position on sacramental equality has biblical integrity, that it conforms to what is reliable in Christian tradition, and that it accords with reason. Indeed, as Richard Hooker intended, we shall be reasoning about the Bible and about our tradition.

For the reader for whom Richard Hooker (1554–1600) may not be a household name, he was the English Reformation theologian who in *The Laws of Ecclesiastical Polity* developed

a distinctly Anglican path through the fracas between Rome —
who insisted that church tradition (the papacy, for example)
trumped every other consideration — and the local Puritans
and continental Reformers who insisted that the Bible alone
was the sole authority in matters of faith, morals, and (increas-
ingly) church order.

Hooker agreed with the Protestants that papal abuses dem-
onstrated that tradition alone is an unsafe authority. He agreed
with the Romans that the scripture alone was unworkable and
vulnerable to subjective interpretation.

Therefore, he proposed a "threefold cord not easily broken"
comprising scripture, church (tradition), and reason. While
Rome demonstrates daily the corruptibility of tradition and
the various Protestant denominations demonstrate daily the
awkwardly unworkable nature of the *sola scriptura* position,
Anglicans have managed to muddle through using Hooker's
threefold cord.[1]

Hooker knew that the Bible was vast, complex, and multi-
layered. To apply it reliably meant you had to use your noggin.
You had to do so in full awareness of what previous Christian generations had undertaken — without servilely assuming
that anything in the past was preferable to the novelties of
the present. You also had to use a heart melted and reshaped
in the crucible and on the anvil of prayer. The combined use
of the head, the heart, and the spirit composed what Hooker
understood by reason.

Trying to be a loyal Anglican I've structured this discussion
to examine sacramental equality in the light of scripture and

---

1. At least we did until the most recent Lambeth Conference when a
majority of the bishops assembled turned away from Hooker and embraced
sola scriptura.

24

tradition as focused by reason. As Hooker would have wished and predicted, the discussion of scripture is by far the longest and most detailed. Tradition is deservedly the briefest. Reason comes behind scripture in size and influence.

Though Hooker himself preferred a different order (scripture, reason, and church — i.e., tradition) I address them in their more recent conventional order. Scripture comes in for the severest misuse these days, so we must consider it first. Tradition is also being misused, so we'll glance at it next. The brevity of that discussion reflects the reality that the quarrel in the Episcopal Church is getting waged on scriptural more than historical grounds. In discussing reason, we have to employ that faculty to understand why our decades-long conversations have produced so little mutual understanding or respect.

In addressing friends and attempting to deepen our discussions and perhaps enrich our proclamations, in the next chapters I am putting some thoughts into play that may not be familiar to most readers. At any rate they are considerations we do not often hear voiced.

In discussing scripture I'll acquaint readers with the fruits of recent researches in several fields that indicate that our whole apprehension of sex and sexuality has undergone so radical a shift in recent centuries that we simply no longer get what the biblical writers thought they were talking about when discussing sex. Phrased technically, the means and norms of gender construction in the ancient world differed markedly from our own. If we could stand Moses and Paul before us and congratulate (or fuss at) them for their condemnation of homosexuality, they would almost certainly stare at us in blank incomprehension. Homosexuality per se simply isn't anything they'd ever been aware of. No kidding.

In discussing tradition, I examine the necessarily political nature of tradition — who decides what tradition is and what it is not — and why. It's important to grasp the connection between tradition and privilege — and to consider how easily privilege elides into an addictive process. I examine some essentially Anglican traditions that we are in peril of jettisoning.

Discussing reason I (as gently as possible) insert developmental considerations into the differences between liberals and Evangelicals with suggestions about how both sides might meet one another on a common level of values-maturity.

Meanwhile, a couple of additional considerations may help our discussions.

A number of years ago I read an interview with the Lutheran sociologist Peter Berger. In it he complained something like, "The church today is telling the world, 'Speak up; you have our attention; we're listening.' But 'listening' is not the church's job. The church's job is to *proclaim.*"

You may or may not agree that proclamation is the church's primary job. But Berger was onto something that could alert us to why our talk for the last three decades has not been more satisfactory. That is, liberals really do like to listen — or at least we like to appear to. The overwhelming number of attempts to initiate "dialogue" in the church emerges from the liberal camp. That fact alone makes Evangelicals and other sacramental conservatives cautious, sensing that dialogue is merely a delaying tactic until the so-called liberal media and Hollywood have nudged public sentiment about homosexual people leftward. Let every liberal reading this think long and hard before saying that's entirely wrong.

Evangelicals evidently read the same interview and agreed with Berger, because Evangelicals delight to proclaim — relentlessly. And knowing proclamation is faithful compliance with the gospel commission, Evangelicals award themselves self-approval points for proclaiming, in season and out of season; the stiffer the resistance, the better. Liberals get tired of listening to *that.*

Right there we can see part of the contour of our talk problem. One side enjoys making speeches and sermons. One side enjoys sitting with others in lengthy conversation in the hope that the "drift to the middle" may eventually generate consensus. One side wants the church to hold up an uncompromised standard of God's requirement for human individuals and society, refusing to bend to the winds of Zeitgeist. The other side wants the church to be a place of refreshment for those who are weary and heavy-laden, a place to meet the one whose yoke is easy and whose burden is light. I know of no single congregation, including my own, that combines those two valuable tasks harmoniously — a good reason for us to stay in alliance with one another.

As long as we are to be blessed by Evangelical proclamations, it would be fruitful if their proclamations could take into account some of the thoughts we'll shortly be considering, so they'll be talking about stuff the rest of us liberals are interested in and actually worry about. As long as liberals have the fortitude of fanny for all those dialogues, we could take more pains so that the topics we select scratch Evangelicals where they actually itch.

Peter Berger made another trenchant observation that ought to help our discussions.

In his book *The Sacred Canopy* Berger retrieved two helpful notions from Karl Marx's sociological thinking: "reification" and "alienation."[2] Reification is using a concept so often that it comes to be a distinct "thing" to us, something that's really there, a piece of our minds' furniture. Alienation here means the state of remaining unaware of how much of our mental furniture consists of reifications and consequently being unaware of their arbitrary quality.

Let me give you an example of "reification" (*thing*-ification, if you will). Years ago I was preparing a couple for marriage. One day the bride-to-be came to me in distress to complain about the groom-to-be. It seems they had made a weekend trip together from which she returned angry and frightened. I asked what had happened. "The trip was most destructive to our relationship," she replied, as though that should explain it. It didn't. So I repeated the question. Back came something like, "Relationship-wise, it was not a constructive trip." Several more volleys produced pretty much the same answer. I never did learn what the specific trouble was — and my imagination went to work luridly. Her insistence that something called a "trip" had caused damage to something called a "relationship" kept her at a distance from any helpful examination of who did what and to whom.

During that conversation it hit me that there is no such *thing* as a "relationship" per se. But there is such a thing as two people behaving in various ways in response to which their companions feel unsafe. There is no such thing as a "trip." There is such a thing as two people close together in a car and motel rooms for many hours at a time, long enough for their courtship manners to slip. She and I were inadvertently demonstrating that there's

---

2. Peter L. Berger, *The Sacred Canopy: Elements of a Sociological Theory of Religion* (New York: Doubleday/Anchor Books, 1967).

no such thing as a "conversation," at least not that day — only two people in the same space taking turns talking. Years later, as I read Berger, that frustrating meeting returned to memory.

Bandler and Grinder's treatment of Noam Chomsky's ideas of "deep structure" within speech in *The Structure of Magic Volume I* shows us something called a "nominalization." The two psychologists seized on the notion as therapeutically interesting because it's a clue that the speaker doesn't know — or want to know — what she's really talking about. Again, nominalization is pretty close to what Marx and Berger call reification. C. S. Lewis used to stigmatize such sloppy if expedient clumping of discrete phenomena as "hypostatized abstract nouns."

Now right away we know we can hardly do without abstractions. Abstract nouns save time. When we talk of justice, that's a lot more efficient than listing all the people we can think of who need a fair trial; when we speak of liberty, we can't list all the people who need release from servitude to specific masters. But the peril of using abstractions is that they become real "things" in our minds, part of the furniture. They get reified. When that happens, we have lost sight of their component contents and their necessarily arbitrary character. We lose touch with what they have no room to include. Grasping an abstraction-turned-reification, I forget to remind myself, "I could conceive of this stuff in some additional ways; it could be otherwise; other hypotheses could accommodate additional data." Now I can brandish my reifications at you and really believe that I'm talking about something that's there.

I was once amazed at a preacher's gleeful self-approval as he regaled us with the proclamation, "We can have *his* righteousness!" (Jesus's righteousness — I think), which he managed to repeat many times without illustration or ever getting around to explaining why that should thrill us. The phrase, "a bloodless ballet of impalpable categories" came to mind. (So one clue that I'm caught in reification is that I sound proud of myself.)

When I start doing that a lot, Berger calls me "alienated." Reification has replaced consciousness. Berger admits that it's too late to retrieve alienation from its current meaning, a synonym for estrangement. But he goes on to use it for the sake of historical accuracy and suggests that we do the same. An alienated person is one who, like the weeping bride-to-be in my office, has lost sight of the fact that she isn't talking about anything palpable. Alienated discussions based on comparative reifications tend to be fruitless.

Berger does not think we begin life alienation-free and only get alienated by degrees. By the time we're consciously talking about stuff, we're well into alienation. The developmental task before each of us, according to Berger, is gradually to de-alienate. We need to be good sports about the places where our symbolic carpets don't completely stretch to cover our actual floorboards. We do that as we spot ourselves employing reifications and decide to unpack them, pulling out the specific elements that make up our "black box" concepts and wondering if they can be arranged and understood differently. That's hard work.

One reason our last three-decades-long discussion has been so fruitless is that it has been choked with reifications.

"Homosexuality" is a reification; the reality is more multi-faceted — and historically fluid — than the single word allows or acknowledges. Our discussions rarely take into account how recent this concept, let alone the reification, is — or what that fact means.

It follows that "heterosexuality" is equally a reification.

So is "marriage." How can I be confident I know what you mean when we talk of marriage, especially when you say, "traditional marriage"?

"Tradition" is a reification. Frequently it means anything in the past that the speaker likes or dislikes — and the speaker is not always aware of that.

So is "the biblical view of..." — well, of anything at all. So vast, complex, and multivocal is the Bible that any claim about a single "biblical" view of something verges on disrespect, however unintended.

In another chapter I suggest that "canonical interpretations" get fixed onto particular parts of the Bible and from thenceforth become the sum and substance of what those passages mean. That's how you reify a Bible passage. If you don't know you're doing it, you're alienated.[3]

"Sex" is a reification, God knows. I blush at the thought of how you and I could ascertain that we're talking about the same thing when we discuss sex.

Our notions of gender and sexuality today are mired in reification.

"Nature" is a reification for us as perhaps it was not for Paul. "What's natural" is a dangerous phrase to use around people who read Berger. It marks you as alienated.

"Orthodoxy" is another reification. That notion had a dubious birth, as we shall see.

---

3. "Love your neighbor as yourself" has been reified in my sector of the church. It has become a counsel of self-love by dint of countless discussions in which people point out, "You can't love your neighbor as *yourself* until you actually love yourself." Fine. But that reified truism directs attention away from neighbor.

By the end of this book "sacramental equality" bids fair to be a reification if I'm not careful. In the following pages, I may slide into meaning "You and I ought to be in favor of everything gay we can think of," unless you catch me at it.

I was once in conversation with a woman who ventured something like the following statement: "I'm, like, an Evangelical, like, 'He-is-no-fool-who-exchanges-that-which-he-cannot-keep-in-exchange-for-that-which-he-cannot-lose' sort of thing, you know?" She had compacted a whole sentence containing a complex thought requiring careful examination into something between a noun and an adjective, a clumped-up gestalt in her cranium. The late missionary-martyr Jim Elliot's observation, for all of her agreement with it, deserved better.

You get the idea.

Could we attempt de-alienation in our discussions — or in our proclamations, as the case may be? It is Peter Berger who recommends it, after all. He sports impeccable conservative Evangelical credentials. He writes editorials for *First Things*, that most conservative of highbrow religious journals. To get more conservative than that he'd have to sign on with Lyndon LaRouche.

There's an additional proposal I want to make before launching the next chapter. If reification is intellectually imprecise, when done to persons it can be tantamount to spiritual murder. We sense that when we resist allowing ourselves to be labeled. Calling me a liberal does no justice whatever to my complexity. And how can I call somebody conservative — especially pejoratively — if they once faced tear gas, fire hoses, and German shepherds on the Selma Bridge? Reducing persons to specimens of reified classes removes them from among those present. That violates the spirit if not the letter of the Sixth Commandment.

Years ago I was asked to do a book on how we might all respond to the needs of homeless people. All through the project I was assisted and encouraged by Anita Beaty, who directed the National Homeless Coalition. Among her trenchant suggestions she urged me to alter the title the editor and I had blandly agreed upon: *52 Ways to Help the Homeless.* That original title had a nice alliterative bounce to it, did it not? But, as Anita pointed out to me, "You just turned a whole class of individuals into an abstract category." She was right. The book came out under the title, *52 Ways to Help Homeless People.* When I think of "the homeless" in my head I see lumps; when I think of homeless people I see faces.

In our discussion and proclamations, could we restore terms like "homosexual," "gay," and "lesbian" to their original function as adjectives modifying actual human beings? In no friendships of mine are the friends' sexual orientations their most interesting feature. That includes yours. So I won't be talking about homosexuals. I'll be discussing homosexual persons, gay brothers, and lesbian sisters.

If just the modest suggestions made so far were embraced on both sides of our controversy, even without reference to anything that follows, our discussions would be immeasurably enriched.

Maybe we can talk.

TWO

Scripture

Let me start with a story. Vincent J. Donovan, a Catholic missionary to the Masai people of Kenya and Tanzania, wrote a wonderful book about his experiences entitled *Christianity Rediscovered.* In it he offers us the following report of his attempts to introduce the notion of universal brotherhood in Christ:

> Suppose you belonged to a tribe like the Masai, for whom there was no abstract notion of brotherhood, but only a concrete, specific idea of brotherhood, arrived at by initiation and extending only to a restricted group within a clan line — an age-group brotherhood called *orporor.* It was by no means universal. It was limited to those initiated within a certain time span, generally a seven-year period. This orporor taught them everything they knew of love and loyalty and dedication and responsibility and sacrifice. But it was necessarily limited by that very time, that very space. . . .
>
> One morning while the community was struggling with this problem, I could not help but notice a man named Keriko in obvious pain. I was certain he was ill. But my Masai catechist helper, Paul, chuckled at my concern.
>
> "Are you worried about old man Keriko? Don't then worry. He is all right. You see, for a Masai there is not much need to think in life. Almost everything he learns, he learns by memory,

35

by rote. It becomes automatic for him, like tying your shoes or buttoning your shirt is for you. He learns about food and clothes and houses and kraals and cattle and grasses and women by memory — even things about God and religion. When he needs an answer to a question all he has to do is reach in to his memory and come up with the correct answer. He can reach adulthood without thinking at all. What you are asking Keriko to do is to take the first thought about the Masai brotherhood of the *orporor,* and the second thought about the human race and the God of all the tribes and to put those two thoughts together to make a new thought. That is very difficult work. What you are witnessing in Keriko is the pain on the face of a man who is thinking for the first time in his life."[1]

The point of leading off with that story is to emphasize that talking about how we are to respond to the presence of homosexual people among us is difficult for many of us at all levels — emotional as well as intellectual. Living in a post-9/11 America doesn't help either. We're all more volatile these days and becoming accustomed to looking at each other squinty-eyed. So treat yourself and others gently as you spend time with this chapter. At each point of learning what I'm about to discuss, I found I was unsettled and anxious, resisting any alteration of the familiar world. It's possible you may experience something like that as well. But God is in it.

What I want to do in this discussion has a specific and restricted aim. I do not expect to change anyone's mind about the issues of sacramental equality for gay people. I lack that power. God has that power and will use it as conservatives

---

1. Vincent J. Donovan, *Christianity Rediscovered* (Maryknoll, N.Y.: Orbis Books, 2003), 51–52.

and Evangelicals widen their acquaintanceship among homosexual Christians. People don't change their minds in response to books like this one. We only change our minds after our hearts change in response to loving someone who is gay. But I hope to *engage* your minds. The considerations I offer here have not yet been persuasively countered by those who oppose the church's new direction. Indeed some of these considerations have not yet been recognized. My limited purpose in the following discussion is to demonstrate that a respectful reading of the Bible allows and may, in fact, require a good-faith case to be made for the sacramental equality of homosexual Christians. Those of us who favor the sacramental equality of our gay fellow-parishioners in committed same-sex families are not ceding the Bible away nor disregarding its authority. Many who disagree with us talk and write as though they were looking at us downhill. But the moral plain upon which we stand is at least level. In places it may even slope a little in our favor.

W. C. Fields was visited on his deathbed by a friend who caught him reading the Bible. "What are you reading that Bible for?" he asked. Fields tersely replied, "Looking for loopholes, looking for loopholes!"

Coffee-hour discussion of the Episcopal Church's move toward offering sacramental equality for homosexual persons often sounds like pro-gay Episcopalians have been looking for loopholes — or worse, that we've spurned the authority of the Bible entirely. That makes people wonder if it's really safe to stay in the church with people like us.

I know sort of how they feel. I once attended a production of Beethoven's *Fidelio,* one of my favorite operas. On this occasion the smarty-pants director thought we'd all be edified if he cast the opera not in the eighteenth century but in the mid-twentieth in military fatigue garb as though Castro or somebody like him were the jailer. From where I sat, the whole stage was a brown smear. It was so annoying I couldn't enjoy even the music. Something like that is the experience right now of many Christians who want us both to heed the Bible and to leave it alone.

Americans have a charming characteristic that figures in our discussions: we despise elitism. We resist the notion that reading and interpreting the Bible should be difficult and require the help of an expert somewhere else. We want a lonely salesman in a Midwestern Motel 6 to be able to reach into the drawer for the Gideon Bible and download the full glory of the Blessed Trinity without the snoopy intrusion of theologians and scholars. Happily, such things happen regularly. But that salesman might find there's more to it after his conversion.

Einstein said, "Everything should be as simple as possible — but not simpler." That's true of Bible study. If you read the Bible long enough and attentively enough questions are bound to strike you that the notes at the bottom of the page don't satisfy. Then the help of experts can be welcome.

MY BISHOP once asked me and another priest to address our fellow clergy about biblical authority. I panicked and called Walter Brueggemann, who lives across town.[2]

I hollered, "Walter, meet me at Manuel's Tavern! I have to give a talk on the authority of scripture to other preachers."

Brueggemann shot back, "Are you guys talking about sex again over there?"

---

2. Walter Brueggemann is one of America's most distinguished Old Testament theologians.

"How did you know?" I asked.

"Because that's the only time you Episcopalians ever worry about biblical authority," he replied. "I wish you'd worry about it when you talk about economics."

That authority question is complicated. Every ordained bishop, priest, or deacon in the Episcopal Church publicly swears that we believe the "Holy Scriptures of the Old and New Testaments to be the Word of God, and to contain all things necessary to salvation."[3] Most all of us would sign that again today without hesitation; certainly I would.

There are roughly two parties of opinion when it comes to understanding what we just swore. Here we will discuss the conservative/Evangelical approach first.

Conservative Evangelicals are deeply grateful to God for the Bible. They find its "plain sense" clear enough to live and teach by. They hold it in great reverence. Such people sometimes feel that to read the Bible "critically" is impious and supercilious, the way all of us would feel if we caught the acolytes playing tiddledywinks with the Reserved Sacrament.

Evangelicals are distinguished for the astonishingly rich interpretations they derive in preaching and teaching. In my own love for the Bible I would feel bereft if deprived of their voices. It would be a disrespectful mistake and a personal loss to reify Evangelicalism.

Conservatives and Evangelicals, who largely oppose the Robinson decision and the sacramental equality of gay Christians, believe that the Bible's status as the Word of God entitles it to what is called a "privileged" reading. That is, the Bible

---

3. Book of Common Prayer 1979, 526. Hereafter referred to as BCP.

is to be viewed as self-interpreting; it should not be ranged alongside other literatures or read through interpretive lenses extrinsic to it. It is to be read as unitary and univocal, such as to permit people to use phrases like "the Bible" or "the biblical view" without embarrassment or delay. When a passage strikes us as difficult or discordant, the problem resides with the reader, not with the book. Though most conservatives are far too sophisticated to believe the Bible reached us by the sort of mysterious processes claimed for the Koran or the Book of Mormon, their conversation about "the Word of God" and "inspiration" often sounds as though the Bible reached us through suprahistorical means, making it less vulnerable to historical or scientific investigation than, say, the writings of St. Augustine. That unarticulated sense may also account for its ease of use as a unitary reification. Evangelicals for the most part energetically agree with Article XX in the back of the Prayer Book, which limits the church's interpretation thus: "Neither may it so expound one place of Scripture, that it be repugnant to another" (BCP, 871). Evangelicals usually discourage calling difficulties between two texts "contradictions."

Indeed this strikes me as an Achilles' heel. Conversation with Evangelicals can give you the impression that the Bible's chief claim to inspiration and authority derives from its freedom from error, that "inspiration" is a function of "inerrancy" or "infallibility." Among conservatives, to raise a puzzled question about passages that point in different directions can sometimes get you met as one who attacks the Bible's authority or inspiration outright. Incidentally, this approach makes their children vulnerable to temptation to abandon their faith altogether if they take an undergraduate course in which the multivocality of the Bible is displayed. That's possibly one reason conservatives have tended to be chary of dialogue with liberals.

These approaches to the Bible clearly discourage readings of it that might appear adventuresome. Their inadvertent effect is to cordon off zones of possible interpretation that seem impermissible to explore.

This party has an additional Achilles' heel (as, after all, did Achilles); it is liable to confuse its immediate assumptions about what a passage means with the text itself. The "canonical interpretation" creeps into the text and becomes the "official version." That is a reification of the "he-is-no-fool" variety.

What's a "canonical interpretation"? It's a way of looking at a biblical passage that we've become so accustomed to that the interpretation has become indistinguishable in our minds from the text itself. Alienation, in effect. Canonical interpretation of Jesus's most moving parable found in Luke 15 has stuck the title "The Prodigal Son" onto the story — subordinating the father's centrality in the narrative. It's a lot easier to see what you know than to know what you see. We are more likely to see what we're looking for than what we're looking *at*. That pertains especially to the Bible.

When the Bible has catalyzed reformation and renewal throughout history, it has done so by its *strangeness*, by its departure from what people had presumed it said. Consequently, reading strategies that filter out or gloss over strangeness neutralize the Bible's power to transform us. Martin Luther had thought the sum of the biblical message was, "Be good!" Then he hit some strange passages. His discovery that both Testaments tell us, "The just shall live by faith," launched the

41

Protestant Reformation, energized by Luther's delighted astonishment. The sandy irritant of strangeness forms the heart of many a spiritual pearl, if the oyster risks opening up to admit it. By cloaking the Bible's strangeness under a pall of presumed familiarity, the Evangelicals inadvertently set up a circumstance in which God must employ other means than the Bible to introduce reform, to move things along. If we already knew enough to begin with, that might be okay.

The centrist-to-liberal party of Bible interpretation and biblical authority — of which I'm a junior member — does not "look for loopholes" as it is often accused of doing. Rather, what liberals seek is harder and vastly more important to find than easy outs. We search for the intention of the original writers and editors. What did the biblical writers themselves think they were talking about? Why did they talk about it? To a limited extent, careful study can open those meanings to us — if we're humble enough not to assume we already know.[4] We try hard to get past what we think we know already to find out what we're looking at. One thing we must steadily struggle to get past is the notion of unitary authorship — which is not, my Evangelical friends to the contrary, concomitant with spiritual inspiration. That and much else is called "critical" study. It is critical not in the sense of smirking at the biblical text — it doesn't — but rather in the more restricted sense of exercising discernment.

This manner of study is tough. It demands that we learn something about the languages in which the biblical texts were cast or into which they were shortly translated. And if we

---

4. For example, do we really get Isaiah's point if we restrict our understanding of, say, 52:13ff to a prediction of Jesus? What might have been at the forefront of the writer's mind while writing? What might the contemporary readers have gathered from it?

haven't troubled to learn them — or have found we can't — we have to find reliable folks who have.[5] We need to learn the history of their periods. We have to learn everything we can about the cultural contexts, not just the Jewish contexts but the contemporary pagan cultures as well. We need to learn their literary conventions and the meanings latent in those forms. (Does "and they both lived happily ever after" mean that the rest of their lives were mellow and hassle-free?) We try to sense the unvoiced "obvious" assumptions, the notions so taken for granted that the writer did not think to mention them.[6] We have to pay close attention to (rather than smooth over) what's "strange" in a text, as the strangeness alerts us to vast difference between the ways we think and they thought.[7] We go after the underlying principles beneath various passages, especially when they collide with what seems currently applicable.[8] So faithfulness to biblical principle occasionally requires the setting aside of the biblical letter.

On my office wall there's a Gahan Wilson cartoon of a suspicious bailiff swearing in a supercilious-looking professor type, saying, "Do you swear to tell the truth, the whole truth, and nothing but the truth — and not in some sneaky, relativistic way?" The critical party really does not seek to be sneaky or relativistic. We do believe that it's respectful of God's gift to us

---

5. There are first-rate linguists to be found among conservatives and Evangelicals as well. The differences between the parties do not hinge on who's best at Greek and Hebrew.

6. For example, Jesus's laughter, too obvious to warrant specific mention.

7. For example, why is there no mention of anything "homosexual" in Romans 2? That's a fertile topic for inquiry, not an embarrassment to be rushed over.

8. For example, the uniform prohibition of exacting interest from a borrower.

43

to go after the writers' intentions and meanings before arriving at our own.

A fundamental difference in these two approaches is the difference between inductive and deductive thinking. For those of us who can't retrieve our old notes from Philosophy 101 right this minute, here's the distinction. Deductive reasoning begins with a generally acknowledged truth that is already established authoritatively, approaches something unexplored, and figures that this new thing has to fit into what's already known in some fashion. In short, it moves from the general to the particular. Inductive reasoning regards its present store of established truth necessarily incomplete; it approaches something new hoping the exploration will add new complexity to the existing store. It moves from the particular to the general.

Recently Garrison Keillor celebrated the birthday of Sir Francis Bacon on NPR's *The Writers' Almanac* with this quote:

> [Bacon] spent much of his intellectual life challenging Aristotle's view that knowledge should begin with universal truths. He said, "If a man will begin with certainties, he shall end in doubts; but if he will be content to begin with doubts, he shall end in certainties."

That roughly expresses the centrist-to-liberal groups' approach to the Bible. Trusting that the Bible's authority will emerge unscathed from honest inquiries, that its authority is not something human investigators must defend, historical-critical scholarship explores what the Bible actually says. In such quarters we hear little discussion of infallibility or fallibility, of inerrancy or error; such discussions are regarded as what mathematicians call "poorly formed" — hence irresoluble. By contrast, the "feel" of the conservative party's efforts at biblical scholarship sometimes makes scholarship seem a subspecies of theological apologetics — an urgent campaign to prop up and defend what is already believed. Berger cagily called this effort "plausibility maintenance."

I am composing this chapter according to the values and assumptions of the liberal party of opinion, assuming with all my ordained colleagues that "the Holy Scriptures of the Old and New Testaments [are] the Word of God containing all things necessary for salvation." For members of the Evangelical community I hope this chapter might pose questions whose answers might foster a somewhat more fruitful discussion than we've enjoyed so far.

BEFORE EXAMINING specific biblical passages that come in for usage in discussions of gay sacramental status, we must acquaint ourselves with some critical differences between ourselves and our ancestors. If we don't, experience demonstrates our discussion will not escape the orbit of canonical interpretations. Attention to these differences will allow us more accurately to discern what the biblical writers actually intended talking about.

Although there do exist what anthropologists call "human universals,"[9] some of our currently best-established notions of human nature in the area of sex are not universal either across the globe or across history. That's difficult for us to grasp since we post-Freudians think our current understandings of sex are

---

9. For example, all known cultures see the same colors and have names for them although the portions of the light spectrum are not all that discrete. In all known cultures, smiles mean pretty much the same thing, as do frowns.

basic and hardwired. But they have *not* been held "at all times in all places by all people." In fact, assumptions about sex, gender, and sexuality that for us are preconsciously obvious would strike the Ancients as bewildering—or even nauseating.[10]

The importance of some of these differences is difficult to exaggerate. To begin with, consider that although it's obvious to *us* that there are two biological sexes, until less than two hundred years ago our ancestors knew for sure that there was only *one* sex — canonically male — and that women were an underdeveloped expression of it.[11] One "sex," various expressions. Women along with the rest of the lower castes were there for the convenience of "men," which meant (as did the American Constitution) propertied males.[12] The value of women and of powerless people was extrinsic, measured by their utility to "men." Females were defective half-cooked specimens of a "male" sex. So obviously was this true to our ancestors that virtually every anatomical drawing of the female reproductive system before, say, 1836 resembled a male penis pulled inside out — even if the artist was looking right at a cadaver's exposed uterus. What he believed tempered what he saw and what he offered us to see. He saw what he was looking for, not what he was looking at.

Here's what that means. The assumption of male superiority was much more deeply embedded in the minds of our ancestors, men and women, than we previously believed. (I'll remind you

---

10. That a woman might play the active part in sex, for example.

11. Thomas Laqueur, *Making Sex* (Cambridge, Mass.: Harvard University Press, 1990), 4 et passim.

12. Reread the Ten Commandments very carefully — the whole passages, not just in the Prayer Book (Exod. 20:1ff., Deut. 5:6ff.). What can you ascertain about the one they're addressed to? (Hint: do wives have to heed the Sabbath?)

in the next chapter that this sensibility remains deeply rooted in our tradition.) It also means that when men and women are mentioned together, the writer is not thinking of a symmetrical arrangement; the writer has in mind a human spectrum comprising both strength and weakness. So if you and I bring the egalitarian two-sex assumptions we now enjoy to our reading of a biblical passage containing men and women, we are out of sync with the writer and with what he thought he was talking about.

Now the Bible does not teach that one-sex notion. But the Bible does *contain* that notion all over the place, mostly uncritically, and only a few passages or writers seek to destabilize it. The fact that we no longer believe that about women or poor people — at least most of us don't — can be seen as a favorable postbiblical development along a biblical trajectory.

HERE'S A CLOSELY related difference that is indispensable for our understanding what the biblical writers thought they were talking about when describing anything sexual. It is, if anything, more difficult to assimilate. That is, whereas for us sex difference refers to different reproductive systems, body types, and endocrine systems, for our ancestors sex difference was understood in terms of degrees of social power. Until quite recently sex as an activity was thought of in much the same way that we think of violence. That is, sex was primarily an operation a stronger person performed upon a weaker person for two purposes: gratifying the stronger and stipulating or reinforcing a top/bottom power relation.

Strength and weakness were calibrated not just in physical terms but in socioeconomic terms as well — as we still do. Sex was legitimate and "nonqueer" as long as it was initiated by a powerful person against a less powerful person *irrespective of what we know as the biological sex of the inferior party.* It was neither monstrous nor noteworthy for an upper-class male to assault a male servant or resident alien. Such copulations were beneath notice. It was noteworthy in the extreme — and monstrous — for such a male to permit himself to be used by a female, by a social peer, or by a male of lower status than himself. Social peers did not initiate sex with each other, no more than they would insult or wound each other. Genesis, Leviticus, 1 and 2 Samuel, and Song of Solomon will not yield their full sense to you until you're aware of that notion of sexuality.[13] Neither will the radicalism of Matthew or Paul.[14]

Again, we must be clear that the Bible does not teach that the sex-as-violence notion of gender construction is laudable, godly,

---

13. Though the Song of Solomon is sometimes cited as an exception to the sex-as-power schema, the gratuitous beating the sentinels administer to the initiative-taking Shulammite in 5:7 appears intended to pull this relationship back into the conventions of the time.

14. This understanding of "gender construction" first achieved prominence with Michel Foucault in his three-volume *History of Sexuality* (New York: Pantheon Books, 1978–86), esp. vol. 2, and with Kenneth Dover's *Greek Homosexuality* (Cambridge, Mass.: Harvard University Press, 1989). It was initially confined to the study of the Greek and Roman classics and then to ancient Near Eastern civilizations of the eastern Mediterranean. Only recently have biblical scholars begun recognizing its pertinence to the Hebrew and Christian scriptures. I find the clearest entry into this understanding in the introduction of Judith P. Hallet and Marilyn B. Skinner, *Roman Sexualities* (Princeton, N.J.: Princeton University Press, 1997), and in the succeeding two essays by Jonathan Walters and Holt N. Parker, respectively. The arrangements they find in classical Rome map quite handily onto the Old and New Testament worlds. Michel Foucault, *The History of Sexuality*, vol. 2: *The Use of Pleasure* (New York: Random House, 1985), 84–85, 210–11. Dover, *Greek Homosexuality*, 84. See also Hallet and Skinner, *Roman Sexualities*, 3 et passim; see especially the essay by Holt N. Parker, "The Teratogenic Grid," 48–65.

or normative. Its writers simply assume it — except in the passages we shall explore that seek to undermine it. These notions were usually not thought of as moral or ethical — because they were not thought of at all. The writers would not have conceived of alternative understandings. Yet that apprehension of sex underlies the Bible at all points — especially when our Lord or St. Paul move to destabilize it.

Do we still believe any of that? Perhaps to some extent. Dorothy Parker, when asked what she first noticed when meeting a person, replied, "Whether it's a man or a woman." Cute. It's also almost certainly mistaken. There is one determination that even today we make a split second before determining the sex — and attractiveness — of a stranger: "Is this person big/strong/rich enough to harm me, or is this person someone I can afford to ignore or exploit? Do I have power over this person? Or does this person have power over me?"

Recently, Susan Faludi wrote a comment on an American politician for readers of the *Manchester Guardian:* "The gender gap is really between those afraid of bullying and those afraid of intimacy."[15] Faludi may have known she was harking back to an earlier apprehension of sexuality. She certainly echoed W. H. Auden's astringent, "The two sexes are the strong and the weak." That notion of sex as power-stipulation does lurk fairly close to the surface of our own awareness, as Dorothy Parker's mistake cloaks. For a scarier present-day example of this notion, drive drunk, get arrested, get slapped with a DUI, and spend a night in jail. That night you'll learn a lot about what sex means in raw nature and at previous points in history.[16]

---

15. October 9, 2003: "Arnie, the Humiliator."

16. Recent heartbreaking evidence offers the chilliest indication of all that this understanding of sexuality remains alive and well among certain of us.

AT STAKE in this difference between the biblical period and ours (to the extent that they differ) is not how you or I ought to behave. The difference forces no conclusion on us as to what biblical verses we should heed or ignore; those decisions should be delayed until we know what a passage *meant,* not just what we think, fear, or wish it to mean. At stake is what a biblical writer thought he was talking about when discussing something sexual. Once we're clear about that, we can prayerfully make up our minds about our own behavior.

It followed from that sex-as-violence system of gender-construction that "straightness" and "queerness" were calibrated along entirely different spectra from those we use today. Our spectra — that we assume everyone everywhere at all times shared with us — are male/female, gay/straight. Among us, genital activity with anyone of your own sex, leading to your own orgasm, is "queer."

Various intelligence officials in the Pentagon and CIA grasp that notion quite well even if we don't. Consider this article from the Associated Press as cited on Salon.com on May 10, 2004:

Iraqi prisoner details abuse by Americans
By Scheherezade Faramarzi
May 2, 2004, Najaf, Iraq (AP) — Dhia al-Shweiri spent several stints in Baghdad's notorious Abu Ghraib prison, twice under Saddam Hussein's rule and once under American. He prefers Saddam's torture to the humiliation of being stripped naked by his American guards, he said Sunday in an interview with The Associated Press....
...One of the abused prisoners, Dhia al-Shweiri, has been widely quoted from an *Associated Press story* as saying that he was more humiliated by the sexual abuse than the physical pain. "We are men. It's OK if they beat me," al-Shweiri said. "Beatings don't hurt us; it's just a blow. But no one would want their manhood to be shattered. They wanted us to feel as though we were women, the way women feel, and this is the worst insult, to feel like a woman." (http://www.salon.com/news/wire/2004/05/02/iraqi_prisoner/index.html)

In the sex-as-violence gender-construction that obtained until recent centuries, the basic axis was "strong/weak," with the "man" regarded as strong and the "woman" as one specimen of weakness. Class and wealth entered into the strong/weak spectrum.[17] What was considered queer? Not same-sex coupling per se — possibly because everyone belonged to the same "sex" anyway.[18] It was "queer" if a man allowed himself to be mounted by a lesser person, male or female — the same as if he had allowed himself to be insulted or beaten by an inferior.

That is an apprehension of sex that seems far removed from our current frame of reference, though we can sense its relicts within our psyches. It may well take time to get used to seeing its presence in ancient writings. Nobody assimilates those notions on the first pass. Without requiring you to believe it at this juncture I'll show you how this understanding of gender construction operates in biblical interpretation. Even before you believe it, I must alert you to the fact that a growing number of biblical scholars, working in good faith and out in the open, find those assumptions necessary for grasping what the biblical writers thought they were talking about when they were treating something sexual.

---

17. Recently at a performance of Mozart's *The Magic Flute* I was surprised to discover a vestige of this notion: notice that Papageno is depicted as "feminine": he scares easily and can't control his speech. Tamino's only conspicuous claim to "manhood" is his social class.

18. Imagine being told that it was kosher for you to court blondes but not (disgusting) brunettes. No more did our ancestors distinguish (in principle) between biological male and female. The norm between peers was male-to-female. Exceptions (e.g., female-to-male or friend-over-friend) were stigmatized as "queer." Below aristocratic peer rank, sexual behavior falls off the screen of attention.

An important implication of the sex-as-violence construction is this: In the biblical world there was no such thing as "homosexuality." More startling: in such a schema of sexual understanding there was no such thing as "heterosexuality" either. In fact, we only had clinical words for "gay" and "straight" as of 1869 — and those were only heard in German for several years. The human race used to divide itself into gender identities of "strong" and "weak," not "queer" and "straight."

Let's stay with what that means. Why did nobody in the Old Testament, the New Testament, classical Greece, ancient Rome, ancient Egypt, Sumer, Babylon, or anywhere else around the eastern Mediterranean have a word for homosexuality, homosexual, heterosexuality, or heterosexual? They had plenty of sexual words — whole lexica have been assembled of their dirty talk. And they knew of a number of crimes committed with the genitalia — principally penises. But no collective word? Why not? Because there was no sense that the various activities and crimes employing penises formed a collective category. Our biblical and classical ancestors did not see "homosexuality" as a unitary phenomenon. Phrased differently, they felt no pressure to reify the various misdoings a penis made possible into something called "homosexuality." They simply felt no need for the term. They had words for theft, murder, adultery, lying, and the like — they needed those words. But not homosexuality. "It" was not something they were aware of as a description, an abstraction, or a reification. It was not a class of action — or of persons. To the extent we superimpose our reified notion of homosexuality or heterosexuality onto the Bible's pages, we will almost certainly miss the point of the passages we so violate. Those passages are talking about something quite specific; we evade them by reducing them to generality.

That means that when you and I read a passage that gets wielded against gay Christians, we must always — *always* — ask the text: "What is the specific crime here?" It is never enough to say, "Um, hmm — it's homosexual; that settles it; let's move on." That distances us from the writer. It may indeed be something bad and likely is — but it's something other than "homosexuality" per se.

I'VE READ WIDELY in the Christian literature opposing sacramental equality for homosexual persons, writings that usually resist the thought that sexual orientation is a created given. Robert Gagnon,[19] the man conservatives quote most frequently, mentions Michel Foucault — the philosopher widely credited with starting us on the investigation of the sex-as-violence gender construction — in two lists that occur in footnotes, but he does not display enough awareness of what Foucault was talking about to disagree with him.[20] You need to know when you read apparently carefully reasoned opposing theological and biblical opinions these days that unless they clearly address the single-sex, strong/weak active/passive gender system of the ancient and biblical worlds, their thinking is not current.

---

19. Robert A. J. Gagnon, *The Bible and Homosexual Practice: Texts and Hermeneutics* (Nashville: Abingdon Press, 2001).

20. Kenneth Dover appears in several more of Gagnon's footnotes but does not get addressed directly. Professor Gagnon recently favored me with an exchange of e-mails on this topic. The exchange left me with a warm assurance of our spiritual fellowship — but unconvinced that he has grasped or struggled through the implications of Dover's and Foucault's work. In the future Gagnon may well offer us an approach to this gender construction schema. When he does, we liberals will do well to pay attention.

So how can people say they favor the Episcopal Church's move toward sacramental equality for gay people in the face of what appear to be clear, uniform, and unambiguous biblical prohibitions of same-sex genital relations?

There are two areas to explore. We need to look freshly at the passages that appear to mandate a heterosexual norm and to prohibit any and all homosexual behavior. We'll discover that the standard canonical interpretation of the few passages that customarily get appealed to in our discussions do not survive close scrutiny. The writers thought they were talking about something other than what we either seek or fear. Please notice that we will not be disparaging the texts themselves. It is only the reified canonical interpretations of those texts that we are going after. When we look carefully at Genesis 19, Leviticus 18 and 20, Judges 19, Romans 1, 1 Corinthians 6, and 1 Timothy 1, we discover that they do not pertain to any gay or lesbian churchgoer we know personally. This is hardly to dispute the passages' truth or integrity; they retain both. But it is to say that they are truly and integrally about something different from what we'd canonically assumed.

Second, there are passages we pass over rapidly that leave more room for acceptance of same-sex relationships than our canonical interpretations recognize. I refer specifically to:

- the complicated love between David and Jonathan of which Saul appeared jealous;[21]

- Matthew's (but not Luke's) account of Jesus's healing the centurion's sick servant, a man likely his sexual companion;

---

21. Danna Nolan Fewell and David M. Gunn, *Gender, Power, and Promise* (Nashville: Abingdon Press, 1993), 146–51.

- various positive passages promoting human intimacy, which in principle apply to gay unions as neatly as to straight.

We need a fresh look at those passages, if only to break up our impression that the Bible is an antihomosexual monolith. We need to give up the syllogism that insists something like,

David and Jonathan are in the Bible, and both of them admired heroes that we ought to copy;

The Bible is uniformly anti-gay;

Therefore the story of David and Jonathan isn't as gay as it looks.

To the first concern — a summary of the verses we think of as exclusively pro-straight or anti-gay: the often-cited passages that appear to prohibit same-sex unions don't survive close scrutiny as prohibitions of anything our gay sisters and brothers embrace or practice. But those passages remain true when we pay attention to what their authors thought they were talking about.

In Genesis 1:26ff we're told:

Then God said, "Let us make humankind in our image, according to our likeness; and let them have dominion over the fish of the sea, and over the birds of the air, and over the cattle, and over all the wild animals of the earth, and over every creeping thing that creeps upon the earth."

So God created humankind in his image, in the image of God he created them; male and female he created them.

With our modern understanding of two sexes, each making its unique biological contribution to our offspring as we cherish each other physically, this passage seems an affirmation of an arrangement we love and enjoy: heterosexual marriage, the merrily tumultuous complementarity of wife and husband. Jungians get excited about this passage, imagining that it affirms Jung's notion that every man contains a woman and every woman a man. But the Priestly writer was likely not a Jungian. Back then "male" and "female" were not equivalent or symmetrical. Female meant defective male. Using the words "male" and "female" was tantamount to saying "strong" and "weak." In view of the notion harbored about one sex distributed across a spectrum of strength to weakness, the original meaning was more likely this: that in creating humankind, God created (and is imaged by!) the whole kit and caboodle across the power spectrum, weak as well as strong. It is a radical notion, though we might regret its constituent elements: a God mostly conceived as robustly masculine contains an element of gentle passive receptivity — a notion we won't really see developed in the Bible until we reach Second Isaiah.

Notice that, our canonical interpretations to the contrary, this passage says not a word about marriage. The human race will indeed be fruitful and multiply — much as did the fish and birds in Genesis 1:22. But the notion that this passage restricts sex to heterosexual marriage is ours, not the writer's. It simply does not say it. Furthermore, much is made these days about how God's image can only be reproduced in the complementarity of male and female together. Three considerations tell against that familiar interpretation. First, the passage doesn't say that or anything like it. Second, the next time we see the "image of God" (Gen. 9:6) the two terms male and female are not mentioned. That tells us that when the writer thought about the image of God, he was not compelled to reflect on the complementarity of the sexes. Third, Christians think Jesus Christ is the supreme and perfect image of God; yet unless you take *The Da Vinci Code* more seriously than it deserves, Jesus bore God's image without the benefit of a female consort.

Now if you want to use this passage as a proof-text that God likes heterosexual marriage, help yourself. No critical umpire is looking over your shoulder, and surely God does like heterosexual marriage. I regularly use this canonical interpretation myself at weddings when they let me preach. But in doing so we take leave of what the writers thought they were talking about.

Have we really lost so much by recognizing that this passage tells us that the image of God deliberately embraces weakness and subordination? Does that not prepare us for the Cross? It would certainly inoculate us against Arianism in which the Father is so splendid and removed as not to be of one substance with the Servant Word. Furthermore, Genesis 1:26ff. is a description, not a command. When we make it a command, restricting intimate relations to a single male and female in order to constitute what we've come to understand as the image of God, we collide with equally authoritative passages: for example, "You shall make to yourself no graven image" (Exod. 20:4, Deut. 5:8). That is to say, requiring human relations to enact the image of God is a variety of idolatry. God's image does not require our deliberate ritual participation for maintenance — to assume otherwise is Canaanite sympathetic magic. Given the strict laws in the Torah against idolatry, it is unlikely that the original writers, readers, and hearers thought of male/female complementarity as a normative *enactment* of the divine image, however much it might *reflect* it.[22]

---

22. I cannot forbear to add that I'll send twenty dollars to any heterosexual who recently addressed his or her partner saying, "Hey, Honey — God needs his image buffed up tonight, whadyasay?"

That's a shallow reading of Genesis 1 anyway. At the heart of the *imago dei* passages in Genesis, at the heart of the great Christological hymn in Philippians 2:5–10, and central to the very doctrine of the Holy Trinity, the image of God is constituted not in sexual terms but in terms of loving, mutually submitted reciprocity. We trivialize that insight when we restrict it to a particular gender constituency.

The gang rape attempted outside Lot's house at Sodom in Genesis 19 is not behavior that any Christian, gay or straight, ever approves of. Let nothing in this discussion appear to soften the writer's and editors' manifest disapproval of it. Genesis 19 does not describe the behavior, intentions, or wishes of our gay sisters and brothers in Christ — any more than it reflects those of heterosexual people. The Sodomites in that passage would not have thought of themselves as "homosexual" any more than present-day jailhouse rapists do. The Sodomites would not have thought of themselves as heterosexuals either. They (or the writers who describe them) lacked both concepts. Lot, after all, did not reproach them for being "queer" but for seeking to violate the sanctuary of his roof (Gen. 19:6–8). Traditional Jewish interpretations of that chapter grasped the principle better than we do: the Sodomites were first and foremost inhospitable; they thought it good sport to humiliate foreign guests.[23]

A more chilling parallel story can be found in Judges 19:22ff.

While they were enjoying themselves, the men of the city, a perverse lot, surrounded the house, and started pounding on the door. They said to the old man, the master of the house, "Bring out the man who came into your house, so that we may have intercourse with him." And the man, the master of the

---

23. For example, Ezek. 16:49.

house, went out to them and said to them, "No, my brothers, do not act so wickedly. Since this man is my guest, do not do this vile thing. Here are my virgin daughter and his concubine; let me bring them out now. Ravish them and do whatever you want to them; but against this man do not do such a vile thing." But the men would not listen to him. So the man seized his concubine, and put her out to them. They wantonly raped her, and abused her all through the night until the morning. And as the dawn began to break, they let her go.

In the morning her master got up, opened the doors of the house, and when he went out to go on his way, there was his concubine lying at the door of the house, with her hands on the threshold. "Get up," he said to her, "we are going." But there was no answer. Then he put her on the donkey; and the man set out for his home.

When he had entered his house, he took a knife, and grasping his concubine he cut her into twelve pieces, limb by limb, and sent her throughout all the territory of Israel. . . .

Notice that the mob accepted the substitution. They did not thrust her back indoors, insisting that they were homosexuals and needed a man for satisfaction. Raping his concubine was almost equally degrading to the Levite as being raped himself would have been. And degradation — literally — is what this episode is about. It has been frequently noticed that nobody uses that passage to condemn present-day heterosexuality.

Sex was about power, not about biological gender in our sense.

The prohibitions found in Leviticus 18:22 ("You shall not lie with a male as with a woman; it is an abomination.") and 20:13 ("If a man lies with a male as with a woman, both of them have committed an abomination; they shall be put to death; their blood is upon them.") likewise reflect a period when gender was understood in terms of activity/passivity, strength/weakness. In that period they assigned what we regard as maleness or femaleness according to who penetrated (maleness) and who got penetrated (femaleness). Lesbian sex, because it involved lower-status persons and did not involve penetration or semen discharge, did not compromise the participants' social/sexual identities — consequently the Torah, and indeed the whole Bible, reports no problem with it.[24] This prohibition — that we had been seeing as excoriating "homosexuality" — actually had something quite specific in view. It sanctioned an act of social murder — the diminution of status one forced on another when one treated him as an appropriate target for any sort of violence — sexual, vocal, or physical. Same-sex coupling with a peer or a superior robbed the victim of his prerogatives as a "man," rendering him unfit for further life, and it marked the perpetrator as a murderer, hence a danger to social order. Again please notice that such an action did not belong to a "class" of nefariousness called "homosexuality." For a man to permit himself to be penetrated was a form of social suicide. These murders, thefts, and suicides defiled the purity of the land by blurring categories. The ignoring of class boundaries constituted a category confusion and was the abominable element — not the sex of the two parties. (Other instances of category confusions included sowing two kinds of seed in one field and mixing different fibers on one loom.)

Old Testament scholars associate the rise of the death penalty in the Torah with the intention to restrict private acts of disproportionate vengeance (e.g., Gen. 4:23-24). Social order is

---

24. Rom. 1:26, as we shall see, refers to women acting the dominant role in sexual "usage." It has nothing to do with lesbianism. The latter is a modern assumption.

difficult to maintain in the face of feuding. The hope of preventing feuds likely plays a role in Leviticus 20:13 as well, as the violated male might well have sought revenge against his humiliator.

In a couple of ambiguous verses in Job 31:30–31, the protagonist seems to insist on his own virtue in not sexually abusing male strangers.

> I have not let my mouth sin
> by asking for their lives with a curse —
> if those of my tent ever said,
> "O that we might be sated with his flesh!" —

Whether or not we suppose that "Job" knew the letter of Leviticus 18:22 and 20:13, he was certainly complying with their intention: I have not used my penis aggressively to harm a guest.

Our current understandings of sex and gender are preferable to the Levitical understanding. We know (most of us, at least) that women are fully equal to men. We "respect the dignity of every human being" — poor as well as rich. We know that gay men and women are just that: men and women. A man who loves a male partner is no more a woman than a woman who loves a woman is a man. Today we know that one's sex is not something another can steal or destroy — except surgically. We distinguish maleness and femaleness anatomically and chromosomally — and even that is more ambiguous in some instances than we would wish.[25] So rational citizens of the twenty-first century need not fear what the Priestly writers feared.

---

25. Anne Fausto-Sterling, *Myths of Gender* (New York: Perseus Books/ Basic Books), 85–89 et passim. See also her two articles on "The Five Sexes" originally published in *The Sciences* now available at her Web site: http://bms.brown.edu/faculty/f/afs/sexuality.htm.

Do these passages still apply to us? Of course they do. Their principle remains valid and is now clearer than before. Do not employ sex to humiliate or demean another person or yourself; that is, never use sex aggressively. Those of us who are heterosexual persons do not exempt ourselves from that warning simply by keeping our sexual dealings "straight."

WILLIAM COUNTRYMAN wrote a difficult and flawed book called *Dirt, Greed, and Sex.*[26] In it, he shows that sexual legislation in the Torah/Pentateuch occurs in two different legal codes — a property code and a purity code. In the New Testament, they uniformly embraced the property code and often toughened it. Yet the New Testament never paid positive attention to the purity code in any department of life and sometimes took evident glee in flouting it. And in the Old Testament, the only two pieces of legislation that pertain to what we call homosexual activity fall within the purity code, material that the New Testament had no use for.

Countryman's book is flawed by a final essay in which he gratuitously stakes out positions that in some cases even those who agree with his analysis do not share. He insists that our rejection of pornography or prostitution have no clear biblical warrant. Whether or not that's true, it reduces this book's utility in many church discussions. I called that essay gratuitous because his latter positions do not follow naturally from his previous analysis. Critics dismiss his entire book by excoriating that concluding chapter. But in the literature I have surveyed so

---

26. L. William Countryman, *Dirt, Greed, and Sex: Sexual Ethics in the New Testament and Their Implications for Today* (Philadelphia: Fortress Press, 1988).

far, even those who speak of Countryman with contempt have yet to answer or refute his foregoing analysis.

Conventionally we read the term "abomination" as though it referred to an ethical lapse. But examination of Old Testament passages in which the word *toyevah* is used shows that it has to do with what we'd regard as sensibility rather than what we'd regard as ethics or morality. (Keep that in mind when we come to Romans 1.)

R. D. Laing suggested a thought experiment that gets at this sensibility:

(i) swallow the saliva in your mouth

(ii) take a glass of water: sip it and swallow it

(iii) spit in it, swallow spit and water

(iv) sip some water; spit it back, sip, and swallow what you have spat back. You may be able to do all four, easily, but many people cannot, and are disgusted especially at (iii) and (iv).[27]

That revulsion is what *toyevah* referred to.

The Old Testament itself is not univocal on the matter of the Purity Code. As Countryman points out, neither Jesus nor Paul had any patience with it. Projecting their own xenophobic purity-based sensibilities onto God, the people of the Second Temple Period required Jewish men to divorce their pagan wives; it took Malachi to shout on God's behalf, "I hate divorce." They prohibited "Moabites" from entering the Assembly of Israel — until the book of Ruth pointed out that they'd just written out King David.

For present-day Christians to brandish the Purity Code at homosexuals is deeply, if unintentionally, disrespectful of the

---

27. R. D. Laing, *The Politics of the Family and Other Essays* (New York: Vintage Books, 1972), 92.

Bible itself. And it ignores Paul's manifold observations in Romans and Galatians that Christians do not live under Torah.

In the New Testament, the passage most damning of current homosexual Christians and their unions appears to be Romans 1:18–32. Here it is.

18For the wrath of God is revealed from heaven against all ungodliness and wickedness of those who by their wickedness suppress the truth.

19For what can be known about God is plain to them, because God has shown it to them.

20Ever since the creation of the world his eternal power and divine nature, invisible though they are, have been understood and seen through the things he has made. So they are without excuse;

21for though they knew God, they did not honor him as God or give thanks to him, but they became futile in their thinking, and their senseless minds were darkened.

22Claiming to be wise, they became fools;

23and they exchanged the glory of the immortal God for images resembling a mortal human being or birds or four-footed animals or reptiles.

24Therefore God gave them up in the lusts of their hearts to impurity, to the degrading of their bodies among themselves

25because they exchanged the truth about God for a lie and worshiped and served the creature rather than the Creator, who is blessed forever! Amen.

26For this reason God gave them up to degrading passions. Their women exchanged natural intercourse [*chrēsis*] for unnatural [*para physin*]

²⁷and in the same way also the men, giving up natural [*physiken*] intercourse [*chrēsis*] with women, were consumed [*exekauthēsan*] with passion [*orexis*] for one another. Men committed shameless acts with men and received in their own persons the due penalty for their error [*planē*].

²⁸And since they did not see fit to acknowledge God, God gave them up to a debased mind and to things that should not be done.

²⁹They were filled with every kind of wickedness, evil, covetousness, malice. Full of envy, murder, strife, deceit, craftiness, they are gossips,

³⁰slanderers, God-haters, insolent, haughty, boastful, inventors of evil, rebellious toward parents,

³¹foolish, faithless, heartless, ruthless.

³²They know God's decree that those who practice such things deserve to die — yet they not only do them but even applaud others who practice them.

The canonical interpretation of this passage is that idolatry led (pagan) men — and eventually women — into homosexuality with the result that they caught sexually transmitted diseases and experienced a deterioration of character; therefore God prohibits homosexual acts.

A close — that is, respectful — reading shows another picture in contrast to the canonical interpretation of this chapter. Current applications of this passage against our gay sisters and brothers ignore several major considerations:

- the rhetorical context of the passage (that is, Paul's overall goal in that section of the letter and in the letter itself);

- the specific sin Paul was analyzing;
- the secular cultural context of the vocabulary he selected for his purposes.

First, let's explore the context and purpose of the whole letter.

The Epistle to the Romans was written from Corinth in advance of Paul's first visit to a church in which Jewish Christians and gentile Christians were not getting along. During the reign of Claudius in Rome, Jews and Christians had been exiled from the city (49–54 C.E.). During that dispersion Paul had met and befriended all the Romans he greets at the conclusion of his letter. Some of those friends seem to have written Paul about the local strifes. Rather than side with one party against the other, Paul used this letter to develop an overarching approach to the gospel that challenged and finally embraced both, setting them up for the community life he began describing in chapter 12.[28]

The passage we're considering was his opening volley written to get the unsuspecting and approving attention of Jewish Christian readers in order to surprise them with a challenge. He began with an actual sin — ingratitude to God — that he then shortly surprised them by applying to their party. From that first mention of a sin, he deftly spun a description of behavior

---

28. For much of this discussion I am indebted to Daniel A. Helminiak (*What the Bible* Really *Says About Homosexuality* [San Francisco: Alamo Square Press, 1994]) — especially his location of Rom. 1:18–32 in the context of the whole letter. I differ from Helminiak and side with David E. Fredrickson ("Natural and Unnatural Use in Romans 1:24–27: Paul and the Philosophic Critique of Eros," in *Homosexuality, Science, and the "Plain Sense" of Scripture,* ed. David L. Balch [Grand Rapids: Eerdmans, 2000]) on the matter of Paul's co-participation with contemporary Stoicism in this passage.

Jews disgustedly associated with Gentiles. Modern interpreters have been assuming that disgusting behavior was what we call homosexuality. We'll see. But why did Paul start with mentions of dubious sexual behavior as the outcome of the sin he opposed (ingratitude to God)? Nothing subsequently in this letter indicates that same-sex couplings — or anything sexual — were a major concern of his. If you proceed directly to chapter 2, you discover that Paul had enticed his Jewish Christian readers into moralistically blaming others in order to slam them with a comparable indictment:

> Therefore you have no excuse, whoever you are, when you judge others; for in passing judgment on another you condemn yourself, because you, the judge, are doing the very same things. (Rom. 2:1)

But how is that a comparable indictment? What is he talking about? "Homosexuality" does not appear in his discussion from here on. On the face of it, that is an illogical and strange sequel to a passage we assume condemns homosexuality, is it not? Are we to assume that Paul was turning on his gay-bashing reader and saying, "You guys are as queer as they are!"? That's unlikely — he did not go on to supply instances of his critical readers' sexual immorality. That is clear evidence that whatever Paul was disapproving in 1:18–32, it was not "homosexuality"; whatever it was also had to apply to his critical reader. As I shall suggest, it was highly likely some similar form of *intemperance* symptomatic of ingratitude and idolatry. Paul's disapproving mention of some as yet unclear sexual symptoms of ingratitude to God leading to idolatry was the first term of a rhetorical bait-and-switch; the second term, the switcheroo, occurs at chapter 2 in the passage just cited. Paul got the attention of his Jewish Christian readers by detailing something he knew they along with other educated Romans regarded as loathsome in order to confront them in the next chapter with their own lapses. It is by no means clear that what Paul expected them to loathe had anything whatever to do with what we know as homosexuality per se, male or female.

Before examining the latter claim, notice once more that Romans 1 was not legislation. Romans 1:18–32 contained no advice for the church in the city of Rome or any other. It was a rhetorical device: enlisting the disapproval of a critic in order to blindside him with an accusation of the same misdeed. If we use Romans 1 as legislation — which it clearly is not — we fall into the trap Paul set for his critical Jewish Christian readers. If Paul could have known we'd make law of his rhetorical device, he'd have insisted his lawyer be present when we read him.

In Romans 1 Paul mentions male and female sexual behavior of which he expects his reader to disapprove. But what was the sin? Read the whole passage and track it back. The behavior was said to occur in the course of pseudo-religious orgies in the service of idols. The idolatrous orgies in turn resulted from the previous sin of ingratitude to God. He was describing behavior no one in the church, gay or straight, is drawn to, expressing a sin (ingratitude) to which gay men and women are not more prone than the rest of us. I wish we were hearing as many ringing condemnations of ingratitude today as we are condemnations of "homosexuality." Once again: what "sin" was Paul ranting about? The sin of ingratitude.[29] And notice that the one word for bad behavior that Paul neglects to use

---

29. Helminiak, *What the Bible Says* Really *Says about Homosexuality*, 65–66.

is the word "sin."[30] There are some half a dozen Greek words that get translated as "sin" in the New Testament; none occurs in this chapter.

Now pay attention to the vocabulary Paul selected.[31] Romans 1:18–32 is typical in vocabulary and in thrust to secular Romans' discussions of virtue and shame. Paul borrowed that material virtually word-for-word from secular writers — Stoics like Seneca or the later Epictetus — material that cultured Jews in Rome would be expected to recognize. He even borrowed terms he himself would not choose to use in other contexts — for example, "usage." The vocabulary he used exactly matches the descriptions of lust found in contemporary writings of philosophers and physicians, making it clear that Paul had mastered those philosophic/ethical discussions and understood them well. As an educated Roman citizen, one who quoted classical Greek poetry to Athenians (in Acts 17:28), Paul had a technical psychological/medical vocabulary available for his use. He lifted language from the Stoics (and others) for this passage with a clear grasp of its meaning to Romans of his day.

Let's pause for a moment to take this in. If you read the later writing of the theologian Paul Tillich, you find terms like "ego," "superego," "neurosis," and "repression." If you restrict your reading simply to other theologians, you miss the fact that Tillich was lodging his discussion in the broader American cultural context of an ongoing public discourse about Sigmund Freud's psychoanalytic theories. You can understand most of Tillich without knowing Freud. But you cannot fully grasp

---

30. Nowhere in the Bible is "sin" predicated of a homoerotic act. You are now the first in your parish to know that.

31. The following discussion relies heavily (and gratefully) on Fredrickson, "Natural and Unnatural Use in Romans 1:24–27."

what Tillich thought he was talking about without learning something about Freud.

If you read the theology of Rudolf Bultmann, you will find much of it clear and self-contained. But you will come closer to Bultmann's own understanding if you trouble to learn something about Martin Heidegger and Jean-Paul Sartre, whose existentialist vocabulary and concepts Bultmann built upon.

You deserve to know that the great majority of commentators on Romans 1:18–32 pay no attention to the broader secular discussion of virtuous living that Paul's thoughts take part in. So they do not see the importance of Paul's vocabulary that alerts us that Paul was referring to something rather different from what we'd assumed. This path of investigation is recent. Some pass over the wider Roman discussions on dogmatic grounds. The Bible is God's self-sufficient Word, self-interpreting, requiring no external knowledge for a correct understanding. But by refusing available knowledge, such commentators forfeit the privilege of grasping and relaying to us what Paul thought he was talking about.

First, Paul used an interesting word in verses 26 and 27: *chrēsis*. That word did not mean intercourse or relation as it is sometimes translated. There was not a trace of mutuality or relationship in the word. It meant "usage" pure and simple — and referred primarily to food and sex.[32] Whatever pleasure it suggested was enjoyed only by the consumer or the perpetrator. When Paul first applied the word *chrēsis* he was momentarily still talking about conventional sex between male and female. That in itself should alert us to the fact that Paul was describing

---

32. For once the King James Version is more accurate than modern versions.

a sexual frame of reference with which he was not in personal sympathy even in its male-to-female expression. Most of Paul's own thoughts about sex were far more generous. Compare that notion of usage with Paul's astonishing account of marital mutuality in 1 Corinthians 7, and you readily see that in Romans 1 he was momentarily presenting a conventional contemporary approach to sex, one element of which — *chrēsis* — he himself opposed. Paul never elsewhere used that word to describe intimate relations.

Now let's look at the rest of Paul's word choices and see why they're important. Many of the elements in 1:18–32 were borrowed from Stoic ethical writings of the period. A preoccupation with sex relations that are "according to nature" crops up again and again in secular writings. Interestingly those extrabiblical discussions were not concerned at all about the gender — or sometimes, regrettably, even the age — of the sexual object. (It would not be descriptive to talk of sex "partners" in those discussions; those on the bottom were thought to have little say in the matter.) Those discussions were intent on sex that was cool-headed and rational — not overheated or fervid. Passion of any kind embarrassed the upper classes of that period.

A moment ago I neglected to state that Paul described female homosexual behavior in verse 26. The neglect was deliberate. Did you know that the notion that Paul was describing lesbianism is modern? In the time of Paul and for several centuries after, to say a woman practiced sexual usages contrary to expectation (or "nature") meant that she took the aggressive role in sex with a man, perhaps insisting on the topmost position. Sex was about strength and weakness and status, remember. If not for the weight of recent habit, the burden of proof rests with those who want to find in verse 26 a mention at all — let alone a prohibition — of lesbianism. For women to initiate sexual usage "apart from nature" meant simply something unexpected — almost certainly dominant sexual behavior vis-à-vis some man. We are not told that the women in question took any sexual actions toward each other. Look at it again carefully.

Interestingly, Paul did not stigmatize this male same-sex behavior in 1:27 as morally reprehensible, as sinful, or as unethical — simply as disgusting to people whose virtue systems stressed moderation and self-control. He shared that focus with the Stoic ethicists of the time. Paul used several terms in common with those discussions. Those include:

epithymia	desire (1:24)
pathē	passion (1:26)
enkaiō	inflame (1:27)
orexis	appetite (1:27)
planē	error (1:27)

Those words occur in that very same order in other discussions, notably those of Epictetus, a later writer who relied on writers and thinkers of Paul's own day. Paul's discussion in Romans 1, in other words, needs to be seen as part of a broader years-long conversation that most of us have never heard of. In those discussions, so preoccupied with what was natural and unnatural, the emphasis was always on a *temperate* rather than an impetuous approach to the erotic. They did not question whether or not the desired person might be of the same sex, though happily many explicitly opposed pedophilia. There was much objection to pederasty in Roman discussion, as indeed there had been previously in Greece — but the objection was never that the objects of desire should have been *girls*; rather they objected to upper-class boys being subjected to that humiliation. It cannot be repeated too many times: "Homosexuality" is a modern construct that did not occur to the ancients to worry about.

Now look at some other words Paul used: futile, senseless, fools, impurity, degrading, shameless, debased. Those are the words Paul used to describe the behavior he excoriated. Those are not ethical or moral categories; Paul was quite careful about that. And they too were borrowed. He was using standard language to make his readers revolted in a self-approving way, but none of what he described was actionable. He did not employ the language of ethics and morals until verse 29ff. — a wad of nonspecific first-century boilerplate not especially pertinent to "homosexuals."

How about his description of male-to-male coupling as "unnatural"? Research into the Romans' likely understanding of what is or is not "natural" does not support our attempts to stigmatize gay sex as "unnatural." What he meant by "natural" was what other writers of his day meant by it: it simply meant, "what one expects." Paul also applied the phrase *para physin* to God's action in 11:24, when God engrafted us Gentiles onto the Jewish olive tree — and there *para physin* was an appreciation, not a reproach. (So if same-sex coupling is, in Paul's terms, "unnatural," so is your salvation. If same-sex couplers are perverse according to this phrase, so is God.)

If male-on-male sex was in the case of ungrateful idolaters *para physin,* what was unexpected about it? Parallel discussions to Paul's that used the same words criticized *immoderation,* the lack of self-control that ancient literature so relentlessly regretted. Paul says some men gave up "natural" sexual usage with women to burn with lust for each other. What would a reader in Rome in Paul's day assume he meant? Those familiar with first-century Roman moral philosophy assumed Paul was talking about immoderate passion — immoderate not in its object choice but in its intensity. Men were supposed to keep their heads clear even when sexually aroused. To get swept away by passion was shameful and "unnatural" because unexpected. "Men" were to be strong, not weak. And what did Romans 1:27 mean that these men "received in their own persons the due penalty for their error"? Clearly — to them — it meant that they submitted to the shame of being mounted. Applying this to venereal disease (though doubtless this behavior was a disease vector) or to piles is a modern, politically motivated canard.

Paul concluded this section with a paragraph of standard moral boilerplate, some of which is sinful in Jewish terms or criminal in Roman terms. Look at the list:

> They were filled with every kind of wickedness, evil, covetousness, malice. Full of envy, murder, strife, deceit, craftiness, they are gossips, slanderers, God-haters, insolent, haughty, boastful, inventors of evil, rebellious toward parents, foolish, faithless, heartless, ruthless. They know God's decree — that those who practice such things deserve to die — yet they not only do them but even applaud others who practice them.... (Rom. 1:29–32)

Those who insist that our gay sisters and brothers in the church are conspicuously ungrateful to God, foolish, futile, impure, or debased, or that they are uniquely prone to the actual sins that Paul just described, have simply not bothered to get to know their fellow Christians. That's lazy on two counts: exegetical and communal. It is a claim that barely deserves a hearing.

After entrapping his readers into criticizing pagans who go to orgies and behave immoderately, Paul slammed them at the beginning of chapter 2:

> Therefore you have no excuse, whoever you are, when you judge others; for in passing judgment on another you condemn yourself, because you, the judge, are doing the very same things. You say, "We know that God's judgment on those who do such things is in accordance with truth." Do you imagine, whoever you are, that when you judge those who do such things and yet do them yourself, you will escape the judgment of God? Or do you despise the riches of his kindness and forbearance. (vv. 1–4)

Snap! goes the mousetrap. Their disgust at the immoderation of orgies was the cheese. From this point on, Paul made no further reference to homoerotic behavior in Romans, except for a generic reference in Romans 13:13. The motif had served its only purpose.

So what was the "same thing" that Paul charged these critics with performing? What best fits the bill is not anything sexual. What fits best is a combination of insufficient gratitude to God combined with intemperate passions in other departments of life — evidently material greed from the sparse examples Paul supplies.

Consider the following passages from the end of this letter:

> The commandments, "You shall not commit adultery; You shall not murder; You shall not steal; You shall not covet"; and any other commandment, are summed up in this word, "Love your neighbor as yourself." (Rom. 13:9)

> Who are you to pass judgment on servants of another? It is before their own lord that they stand or fall. And they will be upheld, for the Lord is able to make them stand. (Rom. 14:4)

Why do you pass judgment on your brother or sister? Or you, why do you despise your brother or sister? For we will all stand before the judgment seat of God. For it is written, "As I live, says the Lord, every knee shall bow to me, and every tongue shall give praise to God."

So then, each of us will be accountable to God. Let us therefore no longer pass judgment on one another, but resolve instead never to put a stumbling block or hindrance in the way of another. I know and am persuaded in the Lord Jesus that nothing is unclean in itself; but it is unclean for anyone who thinks it unclean. (Rom. 14:10–14)

Do you think Paul had "homosexuality" in mind at that point? We have been hearing from all sides that in Romans Paul prohibits homosexuality/homosexual acts (in chapter 1:18ff). A fully respectful reading of Romans 1 and 2 together — or of the letter as a whole — would show us something entirely different: Paul is not interested in prohibiting "homosexuality"; Paul is quite concerned to discourage *judging other people.* Might we at some point heed the Apostle?

It is time we stopped abusing the Epistle to the Romans — and abusing others with it.

PAUL USED TWO WORDS in 1 Corinthians 6:9, which the old Revised Standard Version of the Bible translated "homosexual."

Do you not know that wrongdoers will not inherit the kingdom of God? Do not be deceived! Fornicators, idolaters, adulterers, male prostitutes [*malakoi*], sodomites [*arsenokoitai*], thieves, the greedy, drunkards, revilers, robbers — none of these will inherit the kingdom of God. (1 Cor. 6:9–10)

76

Not many fluent readers of Koiné Greek are comfortable with those translations. The first (*malakoi*) means literally soft, overripe or squishy. It's a word you'd use on a black banana found in your refrigerator. If it refers to male sexual behavior at all — and scholars are by no means uniformly sure that it does — the reference was most likely to one who was "soft" on self-control. That translation brings Paul's discussion into line with almost identically worded contemporary essays. Self-control is not under exclusive patent to heterosexuals.

The other term (*arsenokoitai*) occurs only twice in the New Testament and did not occur prior to it, so its meaning in that setting is up in the air. Here is its only other occurrence in a letter that is regarded as second-generation Pauline:

> This means understanding that the law is laid down not for the innocent but for the lawless and disobedient, for the godless and sinful, for the unholy and profane, for those who kill their father or mother, for murderers, fornicators, sodomites [*arsenokoitai*], slave traders, liars, perjurers, and whatever else is contrary to the sound teaching that conforms to the glorious gospel of the blessed God, which he entrusted to me. (1 Tim. 1:9–11)

Conservatives suggest that Paul coined the term *arsenokoitai* to represent Leviticus 18:22 and 20:13 in their LXX Greek version. Those scholars do not explain why Paul was suddenly so supportive of the Torah, let alone its Purity Code, for Christian churches. The context in which the term occurs makes it clear that Paul has some harmful offense against other people in mind. Each of the offenses he lists endangers the community in some way — even greed, which was understood as greed at the expense of others.

Robin Scroggs suggested in *The New Testament and Homo-sexuality* that the term might describe a young man who inveigles himself into the erotic affections of an elderly man in order to get included in his will and abscond with his estate.[33] The contemporary satirist Juvenal condemned such practices. I bet nobody in your parish, gay or straight, has any plans to do that. Because Paul's use of the term is the first we have, we have to look to writers after Paul for a definition, not a terribly certain measure of what he may have meant. Hippolytus suggested that it refers to a man who sleeps with boys. Contemporary discussions reprehended that activity — but as previously noted, they did so for the disgrace pederasty piled on the boy as he approached manhood. Again, that meaning of the word contains no hint of mutuality or love. It was simple exploitation. Your gay fellow parishioners do not behave that way any more than do heterosexual people.

In the epistles that we confidently assign to Paul himself, there are several boilerplate sin lists, all of which borrow their vocabulary from the Stoics and others. Sin lists seem to have been a literary genre. We saw one at the end of Romans 1 — after Paul got past excoriating unexpected intemperate lust. Of the remaining lists only 1 Corinthians 6:9f (quoted earlier) has ever been thought to contain any reference to what we call homosexuality. That makes it difficult to conclude that anything like what we know as homosexuality was a preoccupation of Paul's. If indeed we want to worry about what Paul chose to worry about, we ought to be discussing the sin of greed (*pleonexia*) as

---

33. Robin Scroggs, *The New Testament and Homosexuality* (Philadelphia: Fortress Press, 1983).

energetically as we're discussing sex, since that's the sin Paul unfailingly lists everywhere.

THERE IS ANOTHER QUESTION that those who wield the Bible against same-sex unions would help the rest of us by answering. Walter Wink has listed all the areas of sexual behavior in the Purity Code upon which the Bible comments.[34] These include prohibitions of incest, rape, adultery, necrophilia, and bestiality — which we still condemn. They also prohibit sex during menstruation, celibacy, exogamy, naming sexual organs, nudity, masturbation, and birth control. They regard semen and menstrual blood unclean. Wink lists fourteen of them. Notice that we blandly ignore most of them — Wink counts about seven we disregard. Why do some of us then privilege the apparent anti-gay passages over against the prohibitions we've dropped if not simply on the basis of personal sensibilities? Clearly Evangelical and conservative Bible readers have a schema, a reading strategy, by which to weight one passage over another. It would help our discussion of what's "biblical" if they might share those procedures and interpretive criteria openly. Some candor about interpretive principles would help both sides, I think — and at the moment at least it appears that liberals are more forthcoming on this question than conservatives.

To put the same question in another context: the Bible has much more to say prohibiting lending money at interest than about same-sex couplings (Exod. 22:25 et passim). Ezekiel even calls bankers *toyevah* — abominable (Ezek. 18:13). If we paid the

---

34. Walter Wink, *Homosexuality and Christian Faith* (Philadelphia: Augsburg Fortress, 1999), 37–44.

same attention to those passages that we do to supposedly anti-gay restrictions, our whole economy would collapse.[35] Where is our worry about biblical authority when we discuss economics? This is another evidence that we need hermeneutic candor from the Right before the rest of us cede the Bible to them or accredit them uncritically as our teachers.

I have before me an article in *Seed and Harvest,* a publication of the Trinity School of Ministry in Ambridge, Pennsylvania, entitled "A Most Dangerous Myth — The Place of the Bible in the Anglican/Episcopal Church," written by the Reverend Chris Findley, a recent graduate. In it the writer, with winsome urgency, rehearses the importance and centrality of the Bible in our Lord's life and in the life of the church. His article seems to assume that those of us who seek sacramental equality for gay Episcopalians hold a lower view of the Bible than his or love and respect it less than he. I don't think it's just my liberal lenses, though, that see his notion of "the scriptures" (or, more often, "scripture") as a unified undifferentiated phenomenon, a gestalt, a (brace yourself) reification. Consequently in his encomium to our Lord's reliance on the Bible there is no place to ask why Jesus played fast and loose with Deuteronomy 15:11 ("Since there will never cease to be some in need on the earth, I therefore command you, 'Open your hand to the poor and needy neighbor in your land' ") in Matthew 26:7–11:

> A woman came to him with an alabaster jar of very costly ointment, and she poured it on his head as he sat at the table. But when the disciples saw it, they were angry and said, "Why this waste? For this ointment could have been sold for a large sum,

---

35. That economic question in fact is answerable from a "liberal" perspective: it's an instance in which we have to abandon the letter of a passage if we are to apply its underlying principle into present-day reality.

and the money given to the poor." But Jesus, aware of this, said to them, "Why do you trouble the woman? She has performed a good service for me. For you always have the poor with you, but you will not always have me."

And few ask why we can't find one instance of the New Testament expositing the Old Testament — only casual proof-texts? Consequently his (most readable) article serves well as a war cry but fails as a polemic, let alone as a conversational entrée with liberals, were such his wish.

Will no Evangelical acknowledge to the rest of us the difficulties a devout Bible reader must struggle with? A woman who wears male garb commits a biblical abomination (Deut. 22:5). Who wrote in your Bible authorizing women to wear slacks? What should we do about that?[36] The Torah prescribes the death penalty for cursing one's parents (Exod. 21:17). How is that authoritative today? The principle endures — that is, don't curse your parents — but what shall we do with the letter? How can the polarities in our church get together over the hermeneutic principles that govern this instance? Help. Let's talk.

Job's counselors speak of God in terms that pass muster with other passages like Psalm 37. Yet at the end,

> After the LORD had spoken these words to Job, the LORD said to Eliphaz the Temanite: "My wrath is kindled against you and against your two friends; for you have not spoken of me what is right, as my servant Job has." (Job 42:7)

What I read from Evangelical circles does not show me that their love and reliance on scripture allows us to discuss such

---

36. Recall that wearing male garb was part of the indictment they used to kill Joan of Arc.

dialectics together. Until we can agree on some interpretive norms, some of us will delay accepting their pronouncements on what's "biblical" and what's not. But the conversation remains open from the liberal end, whatever our impatience with poorly focused proclamations. In effect, when we read all those passages, sexual and nonsexual, with an understanding of the writers' original intention, gay Christians agree with them right along with the rest of us. Gay Christians and conservatives are snug together on the actual sexual ethics the Bible professes.

Finally, in answer to same-sex unions, opponents appeal to the biblical passages I mentioned. The scriptures nowhere specifically prohibit what we are discussing: the sacramental solemnizing of same-sex unions or the ordination of those they comprise. That is more than an argument from silence. It demonstrates that committed same-sex unions were not being imagined by the biblical writers when they described matters that they or their expected readers disfavored. They almost certainly knew of none. We know of none among Jews; none among Romans, where two peers could not copulate; only in a few of the many Greek city-states were peers allowed to form pair bonds. What our homosexual colleagues feel called to establish was not on anyone's radar screen back then, not so much as to spur prohibition.

Do today's Episcopalians know enough about the mercurial history of marriage to recognize that little in the Bible pertains to marriage as we currently embrace it? Who among us today favors levirate marriage (a widow's compulsory adoption by her brother-in-law), polygamy, the wife's loss of title to her own property, the casualness with which men could initiate divorce, or concubinage? If the Bible does not speak all that helpfully to our present marriages, what sense does it make to insist that the Bible condemns same-sex unions by its silence?

NOW LET'S MOVE to neutral and positive biblical considerations concerning recognizing same-sex unions as sacramental marriage.

> I am distressed for you, my brother Jonathan;
> greatly beloved were you to me;
>> your love to me was wonderful,
>> passing the love of women. (2 Sam. 1:26)

If we saw this passage in any ancient literature other than the Bible, we would not hesitate to see it as homoerotic. Most Christians reject that view of this passage not on linguistic grounds but on the grounds of our canonical pictures of David and our aversive sensibilities to homoeroticism. Unhappily for such readers, it gets even worse. In declaring that Jonathan's love was superior to that of women, David — ever the politician — announces that even though he had been Jonathan's social inferior he had nevertheless been the superior partner. If that boast strikes you as unthinkable, examine David's disloyalties in most other relationships.

The relations between David and Jonathan provoked Saul to rage. At one point when Jonathan defended David's absence from a feast to Saul, his father roared:

"You son of a perverse, rebellious woman! Do I not know that you have chosen the son of Jesse to your own shame, and to the shame of your mother's nakedness? For as long as the son of Jesse lives upon the earth, neither you nor your kingdom shall be established." (1 Sam. 20:30–33)

The writer's valuation of all this is difficult to detect (as is so much of the treatment of David in 1 and 2 Samuel) though his meaning is clear enough. The reference to Jonathan's mother's nakedness shows that Saul has something sexual on his mind. We're told that Jonathan knew his father had "disgraced" him. Scholars whose Hebrew exceeds mine suggest a maritally sexual topspin to the word translated "chosen." Saul dislikes the relationship. Is it for its homoeroticism? Or, more likely for its violation of class boundaries? David, the subject, appears to Saul to have seduced the prince. That means Saul will not leave a dynasty behind him. Is Saul seen as right to disapprove of that friendship? Can we even trust what Saul thinks at this point, since the "Spirit of the Lord" has been replaced by an evil spirit? I certainly do not want to suggest meanings I myself cannot find in these passages. This is no ringing biblical endorsement of same-sex unions. Yet it is told of David, the most ambivalent of biblical heroes, without the wry tones of disapproval found later in the David cycle. Conservative objections to that reading that I've so far been able to unearth boil down to stressing that it's an "untraditional" interpretation. More about tradition later.

The logic is circular: the Bible prohibits "homosexuality" categorically; this passage is in the Bible and it's about somebody the Bible likes; therefore this passage isn't "homosexual."

Now let's turn to a visibly favorable response of Jesus to a relationship Matthew thought was homoerotic.

When he entered Capernaum, a centurion came to him, appealing to him and saying, "Lord, my servant is lying at home paralyzed, in terrible distress."

And he said to him, "I will come and cure him."

The centurion answered, "Lord, I am not worthy to have you come under my roof; but only speak the word, and my servant will be healed. For I also am a man under authority, with soldiers under me; and I say to one, 'Go,' and he goes, and to another, 'Come,' and he comes, and to my slave, 'Do this,' and the slave does it."

When Jesus heard him, he was amazed and said to those who followed him, "Truly I tell you, in no one in Israel have I found such faith. I tell you, many will come from east and west and will eat with Abraham and Isaac and Jacob in the kingdom of heaven, while the heirs of the kingdom will be thrown into the outer darkness, where there will be weeping and gnashing of teeth."

And to the centurion Jesus said, "Go; let it be done for you according to your faith." And the servant was healed in that hour. (Matt. 8:5–13)

It's easy to scoff at the suggestion that in this healing Jesus is uncritically endorsing a relationship he surmised to be homoerotic. In fact a scoffing sputter is the most specific reaction I have ever heard anyone from the conservative end of our argument offer this reading. But a scoff is not a persuasive counterargument. It won't work forever. And three serious considerations tell in favor of such a reading.

First, such relationships were common in Roman society and not considered "queer" — so long as the two men were not of the same class. That was the case here. If that's a new thought to you, go back and study the Roman poets and Roman political rhetoric.

Second, Jesus's reference to foreigners coming into the kingdom in advance of and to the surprise of the kingdom's proper Jewish heirs appears to be a favorable acknowledgment of the centurion's unconventional status in strict Jewish eyes. (That punch line is missing from Luke's blander, sexually neutral version.) I think that adds force to the argument from Jesus's silence on the topic of "homosexuality." As Jesus did not live in Jewish Judea but in pagan Galilee, he was surely aware of pagan Roman tolerance for homoerotic behavior across class lines.

Third, this story differs considerably from Luke's account in 7:1–10. Luke had called the servant a *doulos* — the standard Koiné Greek term for servant or slave. Jerome later translated this term into Latin as *servus* — again a standard neutral term. But Matthew calls the servant a *pais,* street slang for a servant used as a catamite. And Jerome grasps this well when he translates the term not as *servus* as in Luke but as *puer* — a word that had exactly the same sexual overtone in fourth- and fifth-century Latin. Matthew knew what he was writing about. He shows that Jesus knew who and what he was dealing with.

The blanket assertion that the Bible univocally opposes homosexual relations in any form does not survive respectful investigation.

NOW I WANT to move to where my heart is. That is, I think a respectful reading of the Bible encourages us to exercise the Spirit's charism of discernment over the same-sex couples among us. Where those relationships are discerned gracious, we can claim the authority Jesus gave the church to "bind and release" in Matthew 16:19:

> "I will give you the keys of the kingdom of heaven, and whatever you bind on earth will be bound in heaven, and whatever you loose on earth will be loosed in heaven."

Do you reckon Jesus meant that? Recently the pope said the Roman Catholic Church is not at liberty to discuss or change its mind about restricting women from holy orders because Jesus had selected only males for the Twelve. I wish the Archbishop of Canterbury had suggested that, in that case, the pope return the keys to the kingdom that clink so loudly, misused, and disused at his belt.

The Episcopal Church's General Convention, in confirming Gene Robinson's episcopate, has finally taken the sort of risk with that authority which Jesus entrusted to us.

What other Bible readings favor such policy? First, let me remind you that Genesis 2:18 does not say, "It is not good for *man* to alone." It is better translated, "It is not good for a *human being* to be alone." Do you think that's true? And if it's true, is it only true for heterosexuals? We hear it said that "God created Adam and Eve, not Adam and Steve." May I ask then who you think created Adam and Steve? We are created so as to achieve our highest maturity and fulfillment in intimate community with a life partner. There are exceptions to that norm, for example, monks, nuns, and the celibate. But they no more flout the norm than do lefties flout the norm that most of us are right-handed. That norm embraces homosexual men and women.

Genesis 2:18–25 comes in for a lot of canonical abuse. The details get blandly ignored in order to make points with it the writer and editors would not recognize:

> Then the LORD God said, "It is not good that the man should be alone; I will make him a helper as his partner." So out of the ground the LORD God formed every animal of the field and every bird of the air, and brought them to the man to see what he would call them; and whatever the man called every living creature, that was its name. The man gave names to all cattle, and to the birds of the air, and to every animal of the field; but

for the man there was not found a helper as his partner. So the LORD God caused a deep sleep to fall upon the man, and he slept; then he took one of his ribs and closed up its place with flesh. And the rib that the LORD God had taken from the man he made into a woman and brought her to the man. Then the man said,

> "This at last is bone of my bones
>   and flesh of my flesh;
> this one shall be called Woman,
>   for out of Man this one was taken."

Therefore a man leaves his father and his mother and clings to his wife, and they become one flesh. And the man and his wife were both naked, and were not ashamed.

First, this passage says nothing whatever about "God's plan for the family."[37] It says a great deal about *Adam's* selection of a preferred assistant. God is not disclosing the divine will to Adam. The divine will is to please Adam, not to impose a choice on him. God is experimenting to see what Adam will find suitable. Adam is calling the shots like a shoe store customer wearing out the clerk with trips to the storeroom. That he selects a woman (whom he does not yet trouble to name) is a narrative necessity, because the two need to produce children in the next chapter. But otherwise the stress is on Adam's delight rather than the gender of his object choice. Furthermore, until after the fruit gets ingested there is no reference to sex whatever. The unnamed woman is his servant, not his partner — or lover. Granted, that may resemble marriages you and I know; but can

---

37. This discussion is one of several deeply indebted to the late Gareth Moore's *A Question of Truth: Christianity and Homosexuality* (New York: Continuum, 2003).

we honestly call that "*God's* plan"? To do so strikes this liberal as disrespectful of the Word of God written.

Let's return to God's original musing: it is not good for the human being to be alone.

> To the unmarried and the widows I say that it is well for them to remain as I am. But if they are not practicing self-control, they should marry. For it is better to marry than to be aflame with passion. (1 Cor. 7:8–9)

Look carefully at what that passage says. Paul, who dislikes unseemly passion, concedes that some people will not be able to govern theirs without access to an intimate partner, a spouse. Paul does not arrogate to himself the job of wading through the community determining who has self-control and who does not. Nor does he license anyone else to make that determination for others. Each individual, according to Paul, has to decide that for herself.

Does that only apply to heterosexuals? Much of the Christian objection to what we call the homosexual "lifestyle" rests on our sensible objection to promiscuity. But if marriage were something from which we heterosexuals were restricted, what do you imagine our "lifestyle" would look like? How would you like having some priest — or magistrate — come along and determine that *you* qualify for celibacy? Even if you had received the gift of celibacy, might you not prefer to announce that yourself? Paul contemplates a Christian community that trusts its members to decide such things on their own.

Indeed, this whole marvelous discussion of marriage in 1 Corinthians 7 — the most pertinent to marriage as we know it in the whole Bible — applies to gay people as gracefully as to straight. Though Paul was not a systematic theologian, we can readily extrapolate four values that Paul thought constitute marriage. They were fidelity, mutuality, truthfulness, and permanence. (Nowhere in the primary Pauline canon or in the letters we assign to his students do we find child production as a rationale for marriage; that is a Roman Catholic canard.) Now look at those values. Is any one of them unattainable by gay couples?

In Ephesians 5:32, where the writer has just been describing an ideal for husband-wife relations, we read: "This is a great mystery, and I am applying it to Christ and the church." Why is the mutual submission and trust contained in that high mystery not accessible by gay couples?

The Roman Communion, to its unacknowledged shame, by restricting the purpose of marriage and conjugal relations to child production, has reduced marriage and marital sex to the level of the animals and lowered the spiritual dimension from primary consideration. Calvin wittily ridiculed the Roman Church for talking out of both sides of its mouth when it came to marital sex.[38] We might join him and notice that though Rome keeps insisting that marriage is in some sense a means of grace, Rome has never yet sainted anyone who achieved sanctity simply through matrimonial grace. They don't really believe it. And we won't believe they believe it until they put some

---

38. "There is also another absurdity in these dogmas. They affirm that in a sacrament the gift of the Holy Spirit is conferred; this connection they hold to be a sacrament, and yet they deny that in it the Holy Spirit is ever present....

"...We must now get out of their mire, in which our discourse has stuck longer than our inclination. Methinks, however, that much has been gained if I have, in some measure, deprived these asses of their lion's skin" (Jean Calvin, *Institutes of the Christian Religion*, trans. Henry Beveridge [Grand Rapids: Eerdmans, 1970], Book 4, chap. 19. par. 34).

other marital value ahead of parenthood — as the Lambeth Conference of 1948 did.

You and I stand in the same danger in this debate. If we misuse the Bible to insist that marriage is primarily defined by its sexual constituency — male and female — we inadvertently confess that we think the *relational* constituency is of secondary importance. The shell is more important to us than the peanut. Suppose we were to decide that the essence of marriage is relational — a point the Pauline discussions in 1 Corinthians and Ephesians are approaching — then we would be hard put to explain why committed same-sex couples do not ever fall within that description. Suppose we said marriage is the intersection of the grace of God and human intention to form a life-long union of two people who seek to live together truthfully, faithfully, mutually submitted, permanently? By what rationale would we exclude any number of gay couples we all know whose lives manifest those graces? To oppose that recognition seems tantamount to a refusal to exercise the charism of spiritual discernment — fearing lest we detect God's grace in such unions.

Does the Bible offer us no reliable counsel about sex? On the face of it, much less than we'd assumed. Not that the Bible is silent about sex, but its counsels rest on understandings we reject for good and godly reasons. We continue to oppose incest — but for altogether different reasons than the Bible's reasons; and, unlike the Bible, we forbid incest between father and daughters. We continue to forbid adultery — but again our reasons for so doing are different from — and indeed preferable to — those of the Bible.[39] In the few places where the Bible

---

39. We oppose incest for the harm it does the less powerful party, not for its violation of the paterfamilias's possession of the one incested; we

discourages — it never prohibits — prostitution, the underlying reasoning is morally less sensitive than ours.

I hope to have made at least a case for understanding that the Bible not only does not oppose what we know as homosexuality but does not even recognize its existence. Why does it not oppose it? Again because in a sex-as-power gender construction there is no such thing as homosexuality or heterosexuality per se. Those categories were not on the radar screen — so they were never what was being discussed. To insist otherwise is to squirt our latter-day prejudices into the biblical text, wearing the fig leaf of "biblical authority."

I want to suggest one more thought. If we grasp the single-sex/sex-as-violence-between-unequals gender construction, suddenly Luke's and Matthew's insistence on our Lord's virginal conception begins to make urgent existential sense, something the most liberal among us would be fools to part with. It's mistaken to debate about biological parthenogenesis — that's anachronistic. And it's literarily doltish to ape *The Golden Bough* and range our Lord's conception alongside pagan semidivinities who are supposed to have been conceived without fathers. Jesus's birth hasn't got anything to do with that. What the first and third gospels want us to know is that Jesus — and eventually his Movement — represent the destabilization of that gender construction — because at the level of his very tissues, Jesus has no part in it. And to the extent that we allow Jesus's life to be our own paradigm, you and I in our spiritual rebirths are ourselves virginally conceived. The Prologue to the Gospel of John says as much:

---

oppose adultery as a breach of intimate trust, not as a breach of a husband's proprietary rights.

> But to all who received him, who believed in his name, he gave power to become children of God, who were born, not of blood or of the will of the flesh or of the will of man, but of God. (John 1:12–13)

The notion of the virgin birth is *not* countersexual. It is the beginning of God's healing the world's sexuality in Christ. It is a revolutionary, radical notion; reclaim it from the reactionaries.

The Bible does offer us a sexual counsel so revolutionary that most churches have not yet even dared unpack it. That is, in his teaching, in his exemplary personal dealings, and in his death, our Lord rejected *dominance*, either his own or other peoples'. He neither dominated others nor paid any attention to their attempts to dominate him. He quickly got over thinking he was superior to women — or pagans — when the Syro-Phoenician woman awoke him from his previous prejudice. Look for that pattern all through the gospels. It will take your breath away. With Jesus's rejection of dominance the sex-as-violence schema first begins to crumble.

Some of Paul's most radical teachings insist on mutuality in marriage. First Corinthians 7 would terrify most of the human race if we took it seriously.

> The husband should give to his wife her conjugal rights, and likewise the wife to her husband. For the wife does not have authority over her own body, but the husband does; likewise the husband does not have authority over his own body, but the wife does. (1 Cor. 7:3–4)

So would the controversial passage in Ephesians 5:[40]

---

40. Though likely written by a student of Paul's, it is quite faithful to Paul's radical insistence on women's equality. Read it carefully.

Be subject to one another out of reverence for Christ. Wives, be subject to your husbands as you are to the Lord. For the husband is the head of the wife just as Christ is the head of the church, the body of which he is the Savior. Just as the church is subject to Christ, so also wives ought to be, in everything, to their husbands. Husbands, love your wives, just as Christ loved the church and gave himself up for her, in order to make her holy by cleansing her with the washing of water by the word, so as to present the church to himself in splendor, without a spot or wrinkle or anything of the kind—yes, so that she may be holy and without blemish. In the same way, husbands should love their wives as they do their own bodies. He who loves his wife loves himself. For no one ever hates his own body, but he nourishes and tenderly cares for it, just as Christ does for the church, because we are members of his body. "For this reason a man will leave his father and mother and be joined to his wife, and the two will become one flesh." This is a great mystery, and I am applying it to Christ and the church. Each of you, however, should love his wife as himself, and a wife should respect her husband. (Eph. 5:21–33)

We are so accustomed to assuming that passage commands obedience — which it clearly does not — that we miss its stunning mutuality.

The fact that our tradition does not embody this core biblical teaching about nondominance is one good reason to view what we call tradition with some caution.

A biblical clincher for many of us is the record of the first time the church faced into a struggle like this present one, a struggle to be repeated several times down the centuries, a struggle that always heretofore allowed the Body of Christ to survive as a church, not just as a sect. I refer to Acts 10, Peter's experience in the household of Cornelius the Gentile and

Peter's subsequent success in persuading the Jerusalem church that his action was faithful to Jesus. You know the story. It begins with Peter's hunger-driven vision, repeated three times, in which a spiritual voice drew Peter past his reflex adherence to Jewish purity laws respecting food. He then responded to an invitation to intimate fellowship with an impure Gentile's household — whom he baptized once he saw evidence that the Spirit was at work among them as among the original Jewish disciples. He now had the problem of selling his action to his colleagues in Jerusalem (Acts 11:1–11). The deck was stacked against him. Scripture as he understood it opposed his action: Deuteronomy did not permit the people of God to mix with foreigners. Tradition was against him: the Maccabean Wars against foreign influences were in his people's recent history. Only reason — in this instance comprising personal experience — seemed to support him: the work of Jesus was unmistakable to those who knew Jesus personally. To their great credit, the apostles and elders in Jerusalem knew Jesus well enough to discern that God was doing a new thing. To cooperate with God, they would have to repress their nausea around Gentiles. The Holy Spirit usually helps with that task, if we are willing.

The church was to face a similar issue several centuries later in the struggle against the Donatist heresy/schism just as she became legal in Rome and had to determine what to do about former Christian leaders who had lapsed from the faith during various persecutions and now wanted to return to their former positions. By the Spirit's guidance the church was eventually able — after longer struggles than we've had so far over sexuality — to discern that the Spirit was asking them to abandon purity as an unaffordable luxury if they wanted to enjoy God's grace as a normal condition. To their credit, they permitted the Spirit to do that work among them. They knew our Lord the Holy Spirit and God the Son of God whom the Spirit reveals well enough to make the shift.

The challenge before the church today is to see if we know our Lord the Holy Spirit and the Incarnate Son of God well enough to recognize God's presence in the ranks of gay Christians.

Do we know God that well?

We'll see.

I CAN'T END without lodging a final plea in connection with the Bible. If we love the Bible and read it faithfully and respectfully, we should consider taking an interest in the matters that interested the biblical writers. For many centuries the church and the world have asked of the Bible questions in which it takes little apparent interest. There are many lesser examples that any of us could readily supply. Most of us would think of the attempt by Fundamentalists to extract cosmological and geological data from Genesis as comically futile — if it did not infiltrate our school curricula.

But that's minor compared to the really big wrong turn the church took with the Bible in the period beginning with Constantine and peaking in the Reformation. The church turned away from the topics the Bible treats so passionately in order to press the Bible into service answering a question nobody in the Bible apparently ever thought of. That new, nonbiblical question is, "How shall a soul hopelessly mired in sin dare to stand before a righteously angry God?" And the standard reply, strung together from verses originally devoted to other subjects, has been, "Christ shed his blood for me." Interest in that question has diverted our attention from two related topics about which the Old and New Testaments are centrally concerned. The first and deepest is nothing less than the utter transformation of persons, communities, and whole societies here and now. And the related interest, reaching its peak expression in the career and teaching of our Lord and the writings of St. Paul, is the categorical rejection of dominance, endured or exercised, in any human transaction whatever.

What the Bible covets for each and all of us is the breathtaking inrush of the sense of God's very presence when we find ourselves in a new unity with persons we had previously feared, resented, or despised. But when the Holy Spirit empowers us to embrace our Lord's counsel about not pushing others around or paying any attention to their attempts to push us around, we experience remarkable transformation. From time to time we find ourselves with tear-filled eyes surveying a roomful of people we realize we want to live to serve and whom we'd gladly die to preserve. That was the exhilaration of the Selma Bridge for all its danger and the Lincoln Memorial for all its crowding as Dr. King spoke of his dream. Even Gandhi the pacifist recognized that as the enviable grace available to soldiers in arms. It is the impact Jesus had on thousands on grassy hillsides. It is the quality of community life that Paul talks about so much more than he mentioned justification by grace through faith.

We might enjoy it again, if in their enthusiasm for their monolithic "scripture," conservatives might read again the ringing words of St. Paul to a strife-ridden church:

If the foot would say, "Because I am not a hand, I do not belong to the body," that would not make it any less a part of the body. And if the ear would say, "Because I am not an eye, I do not belong to the body," that would not make it any less a part of the body. If the whole body were an eye, where would the hearing be? If the whole body were hearing, where would the sense of smell be?

But as it is, God arranged the members in the body, each one of them, as he chose. If all were a single member, where would the body be? As it is, there are many members, yet one body. The eye cannot say to the hand, "I have no need of you," nor again the head to the feet, "I have no need of you." On the contrary, the members of the body that seem to be weaker are indispensable, and those members of the body that we think less honorable we clothe with greater honor, and our less respectable members are treated with greater respect; whereas our more respectable members do not need this. But God has so arranged the body, giving the greater honor to the inferior member, that there may be no dissension within the body, but the members may have the same care for one another. If one member suffers, all suffer together with it; if one member is honored, all rejoice together with it. Now you are the body of Christ and individually members of it. (1 Cor. 12:15–27)

At what meeting was it decided that that's not true anymore? That puzzles liberals. At what meeting was it decided that Leviticus 18:22 and Leviticus 20:13 supersede *that*? In the Sermon on the Mount Jesus was fairly pointed about loving enemies. The pastor in me wants to know and join in the pain that would induce godly men and women to spurn those biblical counsels. Even while liberals ask that conservatives and Evangelicals see our obedience to a different call of God through a different reading of a lot of scriptures as the work of ears, not eyes, of feet, not hands, yet part of the Body — and that conservative sisters and brothers understand that liberals plan to stick with that obedience — could liberals at some point count on conservative forgiveness?

This present moment in our church's life offers us the opportunity to get back onto the *real* biblical trajectory through history, back into the mainstream of the church's deepest and most serious tradition: the breaking down in Christ of the middle walls that divide people — which will catalyze the renewal of the Earth as the sons and daughters of God are manifested to the groaning creation.

THREE

Tradition

Tradition is not wearing your grandmother's hat;
Tradition is having a baby.
— UNKNOWN

"Tradition" is one of the reifications we warned ourselves against earlier in order to be clear in our thinking. The word is easily used in ways that ignore its complexity and fluidity. Let's remind ourselves that abstractions start out as a helpful and necessary way to save time; it's more efficient to say "politics" than to list every candidate we know of and all their known actions. But when "politics" gets reified, we forget the individuals who participate in it and we lose its connection with citizenship. We should not permit reification to economize thought. An uncritical embrace of tradition results in what Berger calls alienation. Part of growing up intellectually — and as a citizen — is to de-alienate to the best extent possible.

Before examining particular traditions, let's reflect a bit on the value of tradition and how we sometimes corrupt its use.

Tradition is to communities what memory is to an individual. Memory is a great convenience to us. It is the function that stands between having to figure everything out afresh and having everything hardwired into instinct. Figuring out everything without memory takes too much time. We can't live that way. And even our vast brains cannot store enough information

101

for us to hold reliable stock reactions to all our daily exigencies in preconscious instinct. We would swiftly be stymied by the unforeseen and die.

So we remember.

Anyone who loves the Bible appreciates the importance of memory at a community level. The eucharistic meal that our Lord gave us as a means to stay united to himself and to one another centers in deliberate acts of memory, as did the Passover celebration that precedes it. Both the book of Deuteronomy and the Deuteronomistic History (Joshua–2 Kings) that it introduces treasure the act of memory and warn against amnesia: "Take heed lest ye forget...." The gratitude that the New Testament stresses in so many places rests on memory. Recalling who and what we are and the gifts, vicissitudes, and forces that shaped us precedes giving thanks to God. But here comes the first caution about tradition. Apart from the presence of God, an individual, even with the best memory, will gravitate toward prideful self-reliance and socially corrosive self-aggrandizement. Memory alone does not make an individual good. Superior memory, after all, is the qualification for cardsharping.

Likewise, communities, apart from the presence of God, whisper divine claims for themselves, pretending to be able to bestow or extend life. All communities gravitate toward idolatry, pressing their internal affections or dissatisfactions outward as chauvinism. So tradition alone does not make a community — or a church — good. Think of all the "We've always done it this way" jokes.

What is the difference between tradition and a simple catalogue of past events? Past events simply happen. Tradition must be selected — that is, somebody has to decide that something in the past is to be solemnly recalled and heeded in the present. Who decides?

Someone in a position to do so decides. History gets written by the winners. By the same token, tradition gets determined by people in a position to benefit from it. Traditions nearly always favor the already-privileged by making sure things will stay largely as they are. Thus it emerges that when we talk tradition we are talking politics, willy-nilly. So the question is, whose politics? Lawyers have taught us the question, *"Cui bono?"* — that is, who benefits? Feminists have taught us to add the question, *"Cui malo?"* That is, who is getting it in the neck? Good citizenship requires that we raise both questions in the face of any tradition.

Tradition tends to serve privilege. Marital tradition until recently privileged the male constituents of marriage and favored married people over single people — and both over divorced persons. When we Southerners insist that we're honoring tradition by flying the Confederate battle flag, I doubt we fool many people other than ourselves. Traditionalist male clergy — or lawyers, or physicians, or CEOs — who oppose sharing our profession with women are doing privilege maintenance. At a grassroots level, what is being called "heterosexism" is a specimen of privilege maintenance. In opposing homosexual sacramental equality or, more likely, the "homosexual agenda," I name homosexuality as a vice; by implication my heterosexual identity, which I lifted not a finger to receive, gets to be a virtue. Religiously anxious people crave all the visible virtues they can display. It's like Molière's Bourgeois Gentleman bragging about knowing how to speak prose.

Recent study approaches privilege as an addictive process. When we have it, we clutch it, defend it, and crave more.

103

We resent and fear those who encroach upon it. It skews our judgment. Recognizing privilege as an addiction and going through withdrawal from it results in a vastly expanded sense of personal freedom and existential space. Ask any fully re-constructed Southerner who had to wrestle with his racism or any Episcopalian who'd previously opposed the ordination of women. The outcome is a lovely paradox: a relinquishing of control and a commensurate increase in personal power.

IT'S EASY to overlook the fact that Christian tradition grew up in a bad neighborhood. As much as anything it is the product of the emperor Constantine's need to elevate and empower an authoritative class of men to take the place of the now-ineffectual Roman Senate as a buffer between the imperial throne and the army.[1] Constantine chose Christian bishops as his new senate and elevated them accordingly. But a price attached to their new privilege. The bishops forfeited the luxury of holding disparate opinions, exploring and ex-perimenting with the truth and love of God in their various localities. Constantine convened the Council of Nicea in 325 with the hope that the bishops might make up their collective minds about the controversy between Arius and Athanasius.[2] The emperor's sagacity can be seen in the fact that, though he privately seemed to prefer the Arian position (as did the

---

1. H. A. Drake, *Constantine and the Bishops: The Politics of Intolerance* (Baltimore: Johns Hopkins University Press, 2002).

2. Arius was a priest in Alexandria who, in opposition to his bishop, St. Alexander, maintained that the first two Persons of the Holy Trinity were of "like substance" but not of "one substance." Athanasius was a dea-con who took up his cudgel in the cause of Bishop Alexander, whom he subsequently succeeded. It was a lengthy controversy fraught with political and cultural as well as theological implications.

Roman upper classes), he was willing to go along with the Athanasian majority for the sake of church unity in the service of imperial unity.

The persecutions of Christians in the Roman Empire prior to Constantine are firmly embedded in the church's lore. Our institutional memory has proved more discreet about the persecutions mounted by Christians against others — including fellow Christians — with imperial sanction. It has been estimated that more Christians died at the hands of fellow believers in the century after 325 than in the previous century under pagans.

On any number of occasions since 325, "orthodoxy" and church unity have been brandished and enforced in the service of secular harmony. The notion of "tradition" has allowed us to overlook truth's concessions to politics. Anglicans constantly attempt to wriggle out from under the embarrassment of being birthed in the supposed lusts of Henry VIII. A more seminal scandal in our institutional origins was the Elizabethan Settlement in which church unity was imposed by fiat and force for the sake of the realm. On the Continent the Reformers showed little reluctance to employ state-imposed violence in the service of institutional unity and doctrinal conformity. When the Puritans ruled England it was same stuff/different day. Protestants ought to be as embarrassed as Roman Catholics or Anglicans at tradition-based abuses of power and violence. The only historically "pure" denominations I can think of are the Quakers, Moravians, and Mennonites — each of which maintains a healthy suspicion of the onset of any tradition.

LET'S EXAMINE some of our most robust Christian traditions. A dubious fruit of the rise of "orthodoxy" during the reign of Constantine was the birth of a toxic tradition we might call triumphalism or Christian exclusivity. This is the notion that the truth of the gospel as apprehended by our Christian communities necessarily requires the invalidation of any truth treasured in any and all other communities. So eager are we to claim rightness for ourselves and wrongness for other religious expressions that we routinely project Christian anxieties onto other groups and demonstrate — at least to ourselves — that we cope better. We assume that Buddha or Mohammed proclaimed themselves or are regarded by their beneficiaries in messianic terms — contemptuously ignoring their actual teachings. We assume that our notions of "salvation" or "atonement" are also what they seek — and that we provide them better. Oddly, outside the Christian churches nobody much seems to worry about those matters. The tragic consequence of this self-serving chauvinism is that we blind ourselves from admiring the work of the Holy Spirit when the Spirit is pleased to don a kimono, a longhi, a burnoose, a yarmulka, or a sari. That narrows the scope of our praise of God and consequently shallows out our worship.

One of the most ancient, durable, and consistent traditions of the Christian movement has been something we are beginning to call supersessionism. It was an early application of the triumphalism previously mentioned. Supersessionism — or displacement theology — is the notion that the Christian church has displaced or superseded the Jewish community and synagogue in the purposes and affections of God; we think that when God says "Israel" nowadays, God means us. Judaism remains the straw man in our Sunday schools against whom we compare ourselves favorably. Few Jews would recognize themselves or their faith in our descriptions. Supersessionism underlies the persistent anti-Semitism that stains Christian history. With very few exceptions, supersessionism is to be found in the writings of every major theological thinker from Paul to Bonhoeffer. If anti-Semitism were not a Christian virtue, Ambrose of Milan would not be a Christian saint. Ambrose was sainted for defying the emperor's order to spend church money to rebuild a synagogue that a local Christian mob had burned to the ground. Literally millions of Jews have lost their livelihoods and lives across the centuries in the service of this malignant wad of Christian "orthodoxy." If you feel like coughing when singing, "Holy Zion's help forever and her confidence alone," it could be the smoke of Auschwitz tickling your throat. Some expressions of Christianity quite close to us have not dropped or renounced that tradition yet.[3] If supersessionism is not "tradition," then, pray tell, what is?

From the time of Tertullian on, it has been traditional for the church to assign evil as the special province of women and to project wisdom, self-control, and the other virtues onto men. That notion floats very close to the surface of present-day Roman Catholicism, a denomination whose fealty to tradition has stripped the teeth off its reverse gear and robbed it of the power to apologize. The Roman Church is a rich means of grace to many millions of souls — but it remains more strenuous for women to appropriate than for men.

I was not surprised to read recently that the Anglican Mission in America (AMiA), led by two priests who crept off

---

3. To become familiar with this heartbreaking, near-uniform element in our Christian tradition, see James Carroll, *Constantine's Sword: The Church and the Jews; A History* (Boston: Houghton Mifflin, 2001). To follow up, read William Nicholls, *Christian Antisemitism: A History of Hate* (Northvale, N.J.: J. Aronson, 1993).

to Singapore to get made irregular bishops, announced that it will not condone the ordination of women. *They* know what "tradition" really means. Ask them.

Now many would want to say something like, "That's not really what we mean by tradition; we only mean the *good* stuff." Assuming the rest of us consent to that fig leaf, is it too much of a trade-off to request that such people include their gay brothers and lesbian sisters and brothers as "good"? Others would insist that, by tradition, they don't mean the practice of previous generations but their *faith* as represented in the creeds and in the findings of the four ecumenical councils of the undivided church. Those of us who favor the sacramental equality of homosexual sisters and brothers hold that same faith. Yet many of us regret that those formularies we call the creeds saw birth as fighting words, shibboleths carefully constructed to allow the church to enforce unity for essentially political purposes. Those who subscribed to them kept their episcopal prerogatives; those who caviled lost their emoluments.

Rick Fabian, the co-rector of St. Gregory of Nyssa's Episcopal Church in San Francisco, recently suggested that if we insist on reciting the Nicene Creed in the liturgy, the history and the spirit of the action require that we troop the colors of the nation and the denomination back and forth across the sanctuary while the senior warden publicly tears up photographs of the Mormon Tabernacle. (I'd throw in pictures of the Kaaba in Mecca, the Shinto Temple in Kyoto, and the Shwe Dagon Pagoda while we're at it.) Is that the "faith on earth" the Son of Man hopes to find upon his return? That notion of tradition passes on to us something darker than faith.

It's important to view with careful scrutiny claims that something or other is traditional. People often claim the force of tradition where it enjoys little substantiation in the archives of history. You can recognize a certain type of conservative Episcopalian by her admiration for all things British. She will prove resistant to learning that the accents of western North Carolina are older than the Queen's; English accents sound so much more traditional to her. She may not know that the pattern of the American flag is older than the Union flag; the latter seems so much more traditional. Many don't know that the ceremonial elements of American presidential inaugurations antedate those of English coronations; the British ceremonies seem so much more traditional. Did you know that Highland Scotsmen began wearing kilts only in 1727 once they'd been introduced by an English Quaker industrialist? Maybe that's long enough by now to count as a tradition. Distinct tartan patterns for different clans are scarcely older. A slippery term, tradition. As the sign on a college campus put it, "We have a tradition against walking across the grass; this tradition went into effect last Tuesday."

Few human institutions claim to be as traditional as marriage. Yet even fewer have undergone more traceable metamorphoses.[4] Imagine how you'd like concubinage; or a woman's loss of property to her husband once married; levirate marriage; polygamy; parentally arranged espousals; morganatic marriage; a husband's unquestioned right to philander; marital indissolubility in the face of spousal or child abuse. All of those were once part of marriage's bedrock tradition.

Within the reification of tradition lurks a set of assumptions that run counter to the Bible's most thrilling proclamation: the

---

4. "Traditional marriage" reminds me of my grandfather's ax, the very ax with which he cleared his land; since I inherited it, it has had four shafts and three heads. . . .

reign of God is at hand! If we believe our Lord on that score, we must struggle to recognize that God is presently, centrally, and effectively involved in human affairs. Right now. That's some of what "at hand" means. Admittedly that recognition requires struggle. But those who undertake it find it an illuminating outlook — that is, it brings into focus elements of the present moment our emotional urgencies would otherwise impel us to overlook. Already many decades removed from the events it presented, the Fourth Gospel offers us a speech of Jesus at the Last Supper that alerts us to expect that further revelations from God would emerge as we grew ready to apprehend them. Indeed that has been the case. So much has that been the case that historical theologians estimate that three quarters of the classical heresies were not the radical liberal adventures of current fable — they were stubborn conservative efforts to maintain "traditional" ways of thinking in the face of fresh revelation.[5] A traditionalist view of things assumes that history is the account of how things have unraveled through the centuries, defecting from a previous ideal — whether the "New Testament Church," the Patristic period, the Reformation, or the ways and customs of the previous rector. As Bennett Sims[6] sometimes points out, that view makes all history regrettable. So who's in charge? Entropy? You can say you believe in God yet think as an atheist. Traditionalism is a good way to do it.

In my own struggles with the slipperiness inherent in tradition, I have sometimes resorted to the old saw, "Tradition is the living faith of dead people while traditionalism is the dead

---

5. For example, Arians resisted updating their Greco-Roman notions of a remote God in favor of the more intimately involved Father of Jesus Christ.

6. Retired bishop of Atlanta and founder of the Institute for Servant Leadership.

faith of living people." That's cute as an opening gambit for a detailed examination of specifics. But it clinches nothing, despite my swollen self-approval at having remembered to say it. I have also resorted to distinguishing tradition from mere custom in defense against repressive uses of tradition. For example, I've determined that by tradition (good) the church has ordained people she discerned as God-called, personally qualified, and publicly worthy; only custom (bad) restricts ordination to heterosexual or celibate men. I continue to believe that's true for the most part. Distinguishing good tradition from bad custom, I argue that the deepest tradition of marriage, as the Spirit has guided its evolution, is that marriage is a relationship between two persons[7] consisting of human courage intersecting divine grace; mere custom requires that it be restricted to a woman and a man. I find that a satisfactory distinction. I also acknowledge that it is somewhat arbitrary. One man's (bad) custom is another woman's (good) tradition. I wish it weren't arbitrary. I too long for certainty, for an "absolute" with which to assuage my anxiety in the face of likely being wrong — thus vulnerable to condemnation. But it has not pleased our Lord to bless us with certainty. The Lord seems to prefer faith in God to faith in "absolutes." Those faiths are not identical.

SO IT CUTS NO ICE that the church "traditionally" has not interpreted the love between Jonathan and David as homoerotic. Or that the church has not lifted up the love between Matthew's centurion and his catamite as exemplary. Unlike Caesar's wife, tradition, as a category of authority, is not above

---

7. Two, so as not to dissipate the intensity of a pair by triangulation with a third person.

suspicion. Christian scholars have only been reading the Bible with scientific critical reason since around 1756[8] to 1805.[9] The tradition of the church has been to rest content with canonical interpretations. For eighteen hundred years nobody cared much what the original writers thought they were saying.

In a previous book I wrote:

Up until the Reformation nobody had to worry much about how Christians should read the Old Testament. The Fathers and early theologians had strip-mined it at will for examples for their teachings, finding wonderful allegories substantiating points they had previously arrived at by other means. In fact, the great bulk of Christian usage of the Old Testament was either allegorical or typological, some of it quite ingenious, coloring our understanding to this day.

Now there are no rules against one religious group using the revered documents of another in such a manner — in fact that may be the safest means to withstand their native appeal. It is virtually impossible to find any prominent Christian writing on the Old Testament that takes a passage seriously for its own sake, that exhibits any regard for the intention of the original writer, until the nineteenth century. There was no Christian interest whatever in what the Old Testament writers had thought they were writing about. The tendency of Protestants, whether Lutheran, Reformed, Anabaptist, or Anglican, was to value Old Testament passages only to the extent any of them could be used either to make a (proleptic) point about Jesus or to shore up whatever moral teaching one happened to favor.

In other words, the first three quarters of the inspired, now inerrant, Bible had no *intrinsic* worth of its own. The Old Testament's value was *extrinsic*, serving as a sort of reserve battery to

---

8. When Jean Astruc first reported finding different underlying sources in Genesis.

9. The date of Wilhelm De Wette's Ph.D. thesis at Jena on Deuteronomy and King Josiah's reforms.

energize the New Testament to which it was attached. History furnishes no parallel to a literature so consistently, lengthily, blandly, and authoritatively misused.[10]

Appealing to the canonical interpretations of those eighteen centuries as authoritative tradition is intellectually corrupt. The problem of our uncritical appeals to tradition awaits someone else's full treatment. I would simply want to advise you to learn everything you can about what people call "tradition" so you can protect yourself and those God loves from the harm that so often lurks behind traditional claims.

A YEN FOR reified tradition likewise counsels caution before kindness toward homosexual persons lest we forfeit ecumenical relations with the Church of Rome and with Eastern Orthodoxy. Both of those communions profess to know that tradition disfavors gay people and their unions. It is difficult not to find that position grotesque despite all the loveliness to be found in those churches. If we abandon this current call of God in order to placate retrograde expressions of religious authority, we betray more than our gay kinfolk. We also betray our Jewish neighbors toward whom Rome, Constantinople, and Moscow have yet to apologize for their many centuries of anti-Semitism. We betray our grandmothers, our mothers, sisters, aunts, and daughters — whom these communions pronounce unworthy to represent their communities to God or God to their communities. To submit to ecumenical blackmail from unrepentant oppressors will cost the Episcopal Church its soul.

---

10. Gray Temple, *The Molten Soul: Dangers and Opportunities in Religious Conversion* (New York: Church Publishing, Inc., 2001), 106-7.

Let me catch my breath after writing that. As I count to ten, I recall the extraordinary graces I have received in all three of those communions — though perhaps not always with their full official permission or by their invitation. I recall the glory of the saints they continue to produce and the breathtaking beauty of their artists' worship of the Savior I adore.[11] I want to slap the back of my own hand as my parents used to do when I was being obstreperous. I want to fuss at myself for seeming to protract an exacerbated schism from such honorable expressions of God's majesty. Let neither me nor you, Dear Reader, countenance a self-withdrawal from those expressions of our Lord's presence on earth. So let us clearly remind ourselves that *we* are not withdrawing from the conversation with *them*.

Presently the American Episcopal Church is being quarantined from much of the Anglican Communion because we consented to the election and consecration of a superbly qualified priest to our episcopate.[12] Traditionalists regret this estrangement even as some of them foment it. Does that isolation not matter?

It matters a lot to many of us, myself included. But dare I suspect that the dissolution of Anglicanism may matter somewhat less to God than it matters to us? Many of us who visit other provinces of Anglicanism come back home disquieted, with a nagging sense that something is the matter, the sacrificial hospitality we always receive there notwithstanding. Our

---

11. As I write this to you, I am distracted by the beauty of Arvo Pärt's choral music — Pärt, whose faith survived the Soviet boot. How can we thank God sufficiently for such saints?

12. Disclosure: Gene Robinson and his partner, Mark Andrew, became warm friends of Jean's and mine several years ago under strenuous circumstances that revealed their mettle.

disquiet boils down to the inability to tell much difference between their practice of communal Christianity and Islam. In some of their worship services men and women sit separately even if kin or married. Women do two-thirds of the work and are allotted one third of the protein. Men hold all the positions, do little of the actual work, and eat most of the protein. If their host nations are considering bettering the economic or social status of women — the only hope, after all, for any substantial improvement in the quality of life in developing countries — the Anglican Churches are either silent or vocally opposed. If we continue to suppress gay Episcopalians in order to maintain some sort of unity with such churches, whom else do we betray?

"Orthodoxy" is a reification that comes in for a lot of use these days in our current strife, referring to a capacity conservatives and Evangelicals possess in gratifying measure and that liberals either lack or flout. Since I don't cross my fingers when saying the creed, I get puzzled at not being thought orthodox. But perhaps that's a mercy. "Orthodoxy" in this sense inhabits a dubious neighborhood these days. I keep drawing attention to how a religious group conceives the status of women. That is because the remnant of one-sex/sex-as-dominance gender construction that lurks so close to the surface these days obviously bears on women's status. Our Episcopal brothers and sisters who have styled themselves orthodox to liberals' disadvantage are often found to have made common cause with the Keep-'em-Barefoot-and-Pregnant School of American evangelicalism. I'm not talking about Episcopalians — yet. But the Mission in America, remember, has just shown its true attitude toward women, under pressure from their overseas overseers.

And men like James Dobson of *Focus on the Family*; Jerry Falwell, president of Liberty University; and Pat Robertson of Regent University and *The 700 Club* — all of whom would just as soon not see women enter the workforce — are their spiritual kin at this juncture. Each of the latter men appeals to the homophobia of their constituencies as a fund-raising tactic. Conservative operatives in the Episcopal Church are not far behind.

We would all be on clearer ground, I think, if conservatives would de-alienate around "orthodoxy," unpack it, and show the rest of us what *all* of it means to them. If conservatives for some reason must revise the faith by elevating opposition to homosexual sacramental equality to the level of creedal orthodoxy, we would do well to learn what and who else is in their crosshairs.

THERE IS an Anglican tradition that we are in danger of abandoning, a treasure God has entrusted to us until the rest of the Church Universal is mature enough to claim it. Ironically it is being jettisoned by men and women who call themselves traditionalists. That is our identity as a *via media*, a middle way. If we are the middle, what's on either side? On the one side is papacy/curialism — or something very like it. On the other side is biblicism, which, owing to the vastness of the Bible, must settle on "confessions" for guidance through it.[13] Coming up the middle, the Holy Spirit has used our often less-than-dignified history to shape a church that is neither determined by hierarchical authority nor by presbyterates telling us what

---

13. For example, the Westminster Confessions and the Augsburg Confession.

we must or must not find in our Bibles. Instead we have been directed to become a *sacramental* church, enjoying indeed the grace of a Spirit-inspired Bible and historic Holy Orders — unified not by prelatial fiat or doctrinal conformity, but simply by our resolution to take our baptismal vows seriously and to prepare diligently for the Eucharist.

If a Roman Catholic or a Baptist asks you for the formulae that determine your membership as an Episcopalian, you can recite two formularies, both contained in our prayer book. The first is the Chicago-Lambeth Quadrilateral that spells out who we are vis-à-vis other Christian groups.[14] And the second spells out who the individual believer is before God, the church, and the world:

> Ye who do truly and earnestly repent you of your sins, and are in love and charity with your neighbors, and intend to lead a new life, following the commandments of God, and walking from henceforth in his holy ways: Draw near with faith.... (BCP, 330)

It is those defining formularies that heretofore permitted and impelled, say, Bishops Spong and Jecko to kneel at the same

---

14. Here is its core: Lambeth Conference of 1888 — Resolution II. That, in the opinion of this Conference, the following Articles supply a basis on which approach may be by God's blessing made toward Home Reunion: (a) The Holy Scriptures of the Old and New Testaments, as "containing all things necessary to salvation," and as being the rule and ultimate standard of faith. (b) The Apostles' Creed, as the Baptismal Symbol; and the Nicene Creed, as the sufficient statement of the Christian faith. (c) The two Sacraments ordained by Christ Himself — Baptism and the Supper of the Lord — ministered with unfailing use of Christ's words of Institution, and of the elements ordained by Him. (d) The Historic Episcopate, locally adapted in the methods of its administration to the varying needs of the nations and peoples called of God into the Unity of His Church. For full text, see BCP, 876ff.

altar rail and receive our Lord's Body and Blood shoulder-to-shoulder, despite their glaring theological differences.

Today we are playing fast and loose with that God-entrusted tradition. Voices still within the Episcopal Church are referring to the recent Lambeth Conference as Roman Catholics might refer to a Vatican Council, calling on the Archbishop of Canterbury and the other primates around the world to function as a College of Cardinals at least, if not an outright papacy. We see few statements either from Lambeth Palace or from the other provinces that anyone is paying attention to that threat to our tradition of sacramental unity.

The conservative and Evangelical members of the Episcopal Church are beginning to define our unity as doctrinal and to flout our sacramental unity by withdrawing fellowship from those with whom they disagree. In effect, by making opposition to the sacramental equality of gay and lesbian persons a shibboleth of virtual creedal importance, they are redefining Anglicanism as *confessional*.

If we get pulled off the middle path, something essential will be lost — and the Holy Spirit will reforge it elsewhere at another time among more faithful spirits. We will lose an apprehension of the faith that is open to the *mystery* of things. Under hierarchical authority the curious will often hear a voice saying, "Thus far shalt thou go and no farther!" — but that voice is not the voice of God. Under confessionalism, the curious will be told, "We have it neatly packaged; do not mess with the wrapping!" Under neither will the altar openly welcome explorers upon their returns home. One consequence will be a drift in our worship toward simply rebreathing our own air.

AT THE GENERAL CONVENTION of 2003 in Minnea-
polis the Episcopal Church embraced the profoundest tradition
Jesus left us: the tradition of the Cross, the tradition of laying
down our lives for friends, the tradition of eschewing dominance in our dealings with others. We prayerfully decided to
uphold a newly discovered application of gospel principle in
the face of certain institutional disruption — and possible extinction. *That's* a tradition worth preserving. It remains an
inviting option, open to traditionalists.

FOUR

Reason

*No problem can be solved
from the same level of consciousness
that created it.*
— ALBERT EINSTEIN

Reason is important — urgently so. It ought not to be necessary to stress that. But history teaches us that rationality always requires defending.

A reporter once asked William Temple, a former Archbishop of Canterbury, "Your Grace, the Roman Catholics have Augustine and Aquinas; the Presbyterians have Calvin; the Lutherans have Luther; the Methodists have Wesley; whom does the Church of England have?" Temple is said to have chuckled and replied, "Plato." What was his point? He meant that Anglicanism was born when reason was no longer seen as opposed to divine revelation and got recognized and incorporated as an essential element in revelation. We have Richard Hooker to thank for that.

We met Richard Hooker all too briefly in the first chapter. Hooker felt compelled by the events of his day to reflect on the question, "How does God address the human race?" — or, put it another way, "What is revelation?" A previous generation had been clear about what revelation was: it was whatever the Church Catholic said it was. The church told you what

God wanted you to know — and to do. Within the Catholic Church, reason had been seen as a separate and inferior source of knowledge compared to revelation. Erasmus had discovered repeatedly how little authority the most limpid rationality exercised when its conclusions even slightly discomfited the church's magisterium.

For the Protestant Reformation the church could clearly no longer be the chief vehicle of revelation. The alternative source of revelation most obvious for Protestants was the Bible. They thought that applying human reason in that setting was tantamount to trickery, given that it might distort the reader's grasp of the Bible's plain sense. By and large the continental Protestants were chary of reason; Luther characterized reason as "a whore who will serve any master." The Protestants wanted to restrict essential knowledge of the things pertinent to salvation to divine revelation, but this time it meant the Bible. Reason played little role. The Reformers hoped that they had settled the matter of revelation by stressing *sola scriptura,* the notion that scripture alone is the sufficient authority in matters of faith and morals.

Hooker was launched into controversy in 1585 when the rigorously anti-Puritan Archbishop of Canterbury, John Whitgift, appointed him to the rectorship of the prestigious Temple Church in London. That appointment represented an effort to counter the wildly popular preaching of Walter Travers, a leading English Puritan. Travers, like the continental Reformers, saw the Bible as the sole authoritative means of revelation, the all-sufficient compendium of everything we need to know about faith, about morals, about church and civil order.

In developing his replies to the radical biblicism of Travers and his ilk, Hooker explained that neither the Bible nor the church can be an authoritative source of revelation from God until we apply human reason to them. Hooker was the first influential theologian to insist that reason not be viewed as separate from the Bible and the church's teachings but rather applied to both. Revelation, in other words, was not a self-contained, self-sufficient class of knowledge, exclusive of reason. Like epoxy glue, revelation required both the material itself (the Bible, the church) and the bonding agent (reason). Revelation only occurred reliably as prayerful human spirits went to work thinking about it in communal discussion. If the source of revelation was the one God who in Trinity of Persons determined from before all time to be community, the intended recipients of revelation ought to be godly men and women who form loving communities of discourse. Hooker said,

> God hath created nothing simply for itself, but each thing in all things, and of every thing and of every thing each part in other have such interest, that in the whole world nothing is found whereunto any thing created can say, "I need thee not."[1]

In effect, we are in this together by God's design.

Hooker knew that process was necessarily untidy.

> For as the case of this world, especially now, doth stand, what other stay or succour have we to lean unto saving the testimony of our conscience, and the comfort we take in this, that we serve the living God (as near as our wits can reach unto the knowledge thereof) even according to his own will, and do therefore trust that his mercy shall be our safeguard....[2]

---

1. Cited by Booty in "Standard Divines," in *The Study of Anglicanism,* ed. Stephen Sykes and John Booty (Philadelphia: SPCK/Fortress Press, 1988), 165.

2. In *Of the lawes of ecclesiasticall politie,* Book V, Chapter iv, 1.

He trusted that it seemed accurate enough for a forgiving God. More to the point, he was realistic enough to know it was finally the only game in town.

Anglicanism needs that insight again today. The various voices raised today against sacramental equality for homosexual Christians refer to the Bible as though its power to reveal God's will and purpose floated above the high-water mark of reasoned scrutiny. We have been there before. It didn't work.

AT THE OUTSET of our discussion of reason, I want to be clearly "Hookerian" about a couple of matters.

First, scripture, reason, and tradition are not three separate-but-equal authorities such that, if I don't like what the Bible tells me, I can always apply to reason or tradition for a more favorable result. They are not separately authoritative. Nor are they equal and symmetrical either. Though Hooker spoke of a three-stranded cord and present-day fans of Hooker speak of a "three-legged stool." I think of scripture as a partially buried treasure and reason is digging hard to unearth every bit of it with tradition kibitzing over reason's shoulder offering advice, not always helpfully. If I were a chemist I might offer a better metaphor: scripture and tradition form an unequal compound activated by the catalytic enzyme of reason. The essential point is that reason is indispensable in our current discussions of the sacramental status of gay and lesbian Christians. Without its operation, we can have no confidence that God has spoken to us. That's part of what it means to be an Anglican.

REASON HAS NOT served the church in this matter so far. To be sure, each enclave of opinion attempts to phrase its urgencies in self-consistent form. But those opinions, howsoever self-consistent, rarely escape the orbit of their original enclaves to convict or convince other enclaves.

Prayer would help. Hooker understood prayer to be an essential component of reason. He knew that reason was a function of the human spirit as well as a function of the mind. Certainly there has been a dearth of prayer on this matter in our day. Both liberals and conservatives think the matter is too clear, too settled, to pray about. Liberals appear to think prayer is a distraction from action, a trick to slow us down. We view prayer with the same suspicion with which conservatives view dialogue. On the other hand conservatives tend (in my experience) to think the invitation to pray about whether or not their position is really faithful to God's intention is a demonic temptation to stray from that which God has already authoritatively — not to say infallibly, inerrantly — proclaimed.

Over the centuries the word "reason" became desiccated, reduced to formal logic. We can already hear that happening in the century after Hooker when Pascal remarked, "The heart has her own reasons of which reason itself remains ignorant." Wesleyans who valued Hooker's insights consequently added the category "experience" to the scripture/reason/tradition paradigm. Some of us Anglican purists have remained obdurate and continue to talk of reason with the understanding that, of course, it comprises experience. Purist that I am in all things (inexplicably, debased critics from the lower orders have actually been heard to mutter the term "snob" with oblique gestures in my direction), I want us to consider experience on its own. Why? Primarily because it has been experience that God has repeatedly used on so many of us to change our minds about the sacramental equality of homosexual sisters and brothers.

No church discussion can be complete without some description of how this happens. Only thus can the reader evaluate my claim that it is God at work in our conversions. So permit me to put before you some of my own experiences in struggling with these matters. I think they will, to some extent, substantiate the position I'm presenting to you as the best application of reason. From Hooker's standpoint, these episodes would be part of what he meant by "reason."

AS A BOY I attended an all-male New England boarding school. My schoolmates and I were terrified of homosexuality. "Faggot" was a commonly heard insult in arguments. In fact we were terrified of our own sexuality. Confine hundreds of pubescent boys together for months at a time without girls around, and you produce a tense population. Suppose my burgeoning Eros attaches to my close friend? The best protection against something so unthinkable is the neurotic reaction of hating the very notion of homosexuality.

For much of my life I faced little that called that attitude into any question. In the church, in the Bible, and among Charismatics I found much to undergird it. Even God was thought to endorse our hatred of homosexuals. Opposing gays was a moral free lunch.

Then two events rocked me loose from that opinion. The first was a courageous initiative by the diocesan chapter of Integrity, an organization of devout homosexual men and women and their supporters in the Episcopal Church. Knowing my opposition to them (I was a notorious Charismatic, after all) they invited me to be the eucharistic celebrant and discussion leader at one of their monthly meetings. I agreed.

The liturgy occurred in an upstairs Sunday school room of a downtown parish — the modern equivalent of a catacomb, I guess, since on a Friday night the third story of a church building is likely to remain private. Integrity members had arranged and decorated the spare room with care, transforming it into a chapel. As I stood at the altar, facing the gathering, I recognized a man who once had applied to be my organist. Now he was out of the closet and out of his marriage, reporting that he and his wife were now cordial friends. I was surprised to see a priest colleague there who said to me, "Uh, Gray, we rely on your discretion about who you see here tonight; not all of us are out." Her courage and willingness to trust an enemy reached something deep inside me. As I was conducting the liturgy, I felt the familiar presence:

"Gray, how do your cheeks feel?"

An odd question, but I noticed how my cheeks felt. In fact they felt cramped — fatigued with my rictus grin of false comfort and bonhomie.

"Relax, Gray — look around you. You are in my kingdom."

I looked — and it was so. As the frequent celebrant in front of men and women who love Jesus a lot, I know the expressions worshiping faces assume. Most of these faces wore that expression.

During the ensuing discussion, I was asked to describe Charismatic spirituality to the gathering. I did my best, describing our delight with the deep consistencies we discovered running like aquifers beneath the surface texts of the Bible, our discoveries of God's interest in our healing, our love and admiration for Paul of Tarsus, and the like. I didn't think it was going down very well with this audience. After all, people like me were and remain the most vocal opponents to everything that these men and women are asking of the church. One man remarked, "I already belong to one despised minority; why should I join another?" I tried to suggest some reasons he might consider it. But I was aware that I could not say, "Because we'd welcome you and be so glad to have you with us." Evidently a number of them thought it was worth a try. The (crypto-Charismatic) chaplain informed me later that two men had asked her to pray for their Spirit-baptisms — and that the steering committee had formed itself as a prayer group. All in response to our evening together.

I felt like Jonah, sulking under the dead leaf, furious that Nineveh was being spared. Like Jonah, I knew I had better taste in people than God does. Hearts are conservative organs. It takes a while for them to change. Though I had just witnessed an unmistakable work of God, much like Peter in Acts 10, I remained resentful.

I WAS NOT LEFT to sulk for long. A General Convention of the Episcopal Church was to be held in the summer of 1991, and our adult summer discussion forum at St. Patrick's was discussing issues likely to come before that legislative body. The sacramental status of gay Episcopalians had become a major issue in our denomination almost twenty years earlier, and I was preparing a presentation of the church's standard position, which boiled down to very few words: "No sex outside of marriage; gay unions aren't marriages; so no sex for gay people; sorry...."

A few days before that class, I was praying, asking God's help that my presentation would not ruffle feathers nor get my own tail feathers scorched. Suddenly my prayers were interrupted by the actual presence of God. My Trinitarian discernment is sometimes fuzzy, but it felt like the First Person.

"*Gray, are you aware that my homosexual children are being lacerated by the effects of multiple sexual relationships?*" (I was struck by God's uncritically claiming them as family.)

Internally I replied, "Everybody knows that, Lord — that's part of the problem with those folks. That's why there's all that violence in the gay and lesbian community; that's why AIDS spreads so fast."

"*If I wanted to introduce the grace of relational stability into those communities and wanted to use the sacrament of holy matrimony to that effect, is there a church in America that could hear me make that request?*"

I knew the answer was no. Liberal churches couldn't hear God request that because liberals are already doing it without praying about it — on the grounds of justice and logic, not divine command. And conservative churches would assume they were being tempted by the devil. I was stunned at the thought. Until that moment, it had never crossed my mind that God might actually *want* same-sex unions as a sacramental option.

A few weeks later I was in conversation with a friend in another diocese. He is in most things much more traditional and conservative than I; graduates of Trinity School of Ministry, Ambridge, Pennsylvania, tend to be. I described my sense of God's breaking into my prayer with those questions, asking if he thought that could have really been God. His reply surprised me:

"No question about it. God told me the same thing. I was praying about the keys to the kingdom passage in Matthew 16. Jesus broke in and asked, '*Why are you so chickenhearted about using the authority to bind and release? If you decided to bind gay people's unions as holy matrimony, don't you know I would back you?'"*

I said, "Man, what are you going to do about that?"

He replied, "Nothing. My mama didn't raise any fools!"

But my mama sure did. More to the point, she raised North Carolinians. Tar Heels don't refuse a dare.

IN A CLOSE SYSTEM like St. Patrick's Episcopal Church, Atlanta, there are few real secrets. If my mind got changed about the sacramental status of gay Christians, people would know it before I said anything about it. By 1993 homosexuality was an adrenaline-contaminated topic all over the church, national and local. That summer St. Patrick's devoted the adult discussion forum to homosexuality as a spiritual, theological, and biblical interpretive question. Both the national church and the diocese had mandated such discussions in local parishes. It was our turn.

The planning committee, on my recommendation, decided to base the summer's discussion on William Countryman's *Dirt, Greed, and Sex.* Though his concluding chapter (as he warned in his preface) presents personal positions not required by his previous analysis of scripture texts, that very chapter seemed the only one lots of participants read. I guess they skipped from the preface to see what was so lurid. They found out, for example, that evidently there was no (biblical) problem with pornography. The discussion got off to an explosive start. Before the first session was over, one man in the back of the room who'd read only the last chapter loudly compared me to David Koresh, the late-departed leader of the Branch Davidians in Waco.

Somewhat to my naïve surprise, a lot of audience energy went into smoking out my personal position on the matter, though I stressed repeatedly that the point of this series was an exercise in ethical discourse. This was not and could not be a policy discussion leading to a change in parish practice. Finally under pressure I got impatient and told them exactly what my thoughts were on that topic. From then on, it was open war between myself and a large, well-organized cadre of former friends. When people think they're defending both God's own standards and their children's safety, courtesy and restraint do not appear called for.

My job was on the line. So was the affectionate respect of a congregation whose love I had always taken almost for granted. That's scary for parish rectors. As I had changed my mind as a result of prayer, I naïvely expected others to do the same. But invariably, when I requested that my parishioners pray about it for themselves, they would stare momentarily like deer caught in the headlights — then a flash grin of sly relief would appear: "I don't need to pray about that — I have the Bible!" That uniform reaction suggests that prayer is equally scary on both sides of the political aisle.

Sensing that I was in for a lot of trouble, I registered for an intensive weekend retreat a friend offered, asking for help to work on the issue of fear. The sort of therapeutic work I sought out is scary, sort of "Son of Primal Scream." The therapist, a friend named Harold, blindfolds you, lays you down on a sheeted mat surrounded by other members of the weekend community, gets you hyperventilating and yelling your throat raw. Within minutes you're in a regressed, near-psychotic state. While you're in that condition, Harold puts you through all sorts of physical and mental exercises, intensifying metaphors of whatever issues you're working on. You take a controlled trip deep into what you're most scared of — and back. In that state I confronted the fears that threatened me: job loss and financial insecurity, and (worse) ostracism, exclusion, and isolation by people whose trust and love had always been a staple. As I let those fears catch up with me, it was as though I was in a vast cavern. It was pitch dark and something huge, hideous, and hateful — colored arterial blood red — was rolling ineluctably toward me to annihilate me. I could not get out of its path. It was so utterly terrifying that I felt the onset of a cardiac episode and suffocating asthma.

Harold shouted instructions to me: "Call on some people for help!"

I could think of no one to call on, no one who'd be adequate. Certainly nobody in the church.

"Call on your parents — call their names aloud!"

I did.

Still the thing — death itself — came rolling at me.

"Find a resource!" Harold commanded urgently.

"JEEEEESSSSUUUUUUUUUUUUSSSS..."

"I am here."

DO YOU KNOW the place in Psalm 139 where it says,

> Where can I go from your spirit?
>   where can I flee from your presence?
> If I ascend to heaven, you are there;
>   if I make my bed in Sheol, you are there.
> If I take the wings of the morning
>   and settle at the farthest limits of the sea,
> Even there your hand shall lead me
>   and your right hand shall hold me fast.

> If I say, "Surely the darkness shall cover me,
>   and the light around me become night,"
> Even the darkness is not dark to you;
>   the night is as bright as the day,
>   for darkness is as light to you.

That's every bit true.

Jesus and I held each other in the dark, me weeping like a child with the relief of terror immediately past. I think Harold deduced what was happening and lent Jesus his own form to hug me with and hold me safe. We stayed like that a long time until I was back. It occurs to me today that, to the spectators waiting their turns, we must have looked pretty gay. No matter.

It was now real clear. There would be no resource but our Lord himself in the struggles to come. And he would be enough. If I were asked to string every moment together for the rest of the year in which I experienced active fear, that daisy chain would amount to less than two minutes.

JUST AS WELL. The rest of the year was pretty awful, and it was good to go through it calm and accompanied. Vestry meetings were ambushes, bullfights in which I most certainly was not the matador, my senior warden and I alone standing off angry complainants armed with unannounced petitions. Those who felt tempted to be my allies were cowed by all the vehemence, while those opposing me seemed swept up into some movie script in which each got to play Martin Luther boldly opposing the cardinal. "Liberal" books disappeared from the parish library, stolen by parishioners locally trained by Pat Robertson's people. Anonymous mailings papered the parish, replete with frothy misspellings. Threats ("I'm calling on every member to suspend their pledge payments until you resign!"), recriminations ("Our rector doesn't know sin when he sees it!"), on and on without any letup. For months I was the object of at least two vituperative blasts a day from people who had formerly insisted on how much they loved Jesus and me. Now they wouldn't stand close to me for fear of an inaccurate lightning strike. And that doesn't count the mail.

"Lord, how do you want me to respond to this dear saint?" I would ask several times a day.

"Courteously. Listen for their pain and respond to it. But do not waver...."

And so it would go.

One happy moment between me and our Lord came about as a result of one of several vestry resignations. A vestrywoman who used to barge into my office semiweekly to recite my sins to me visited one day to announce her upcoming departure from the parish. She reported that she felt stumped about how to word her letter to her vestry colleagues. She wanted her opposition to me to be strong and clear. I'd been listening to her objections for several months at this point. So I offered her a summary of what she'd been telling me for weeks. "Would you write that down?" she requested. Because it would not be difficult to recall her diatribes, I replied, "Sure, when I find time," I said, and e-mailed it to her the next day. Later that day she came by, brandishing the printed e-mail. "Is this my stuff?" she asked. "Well, the actual words are mine, but that's pretty much what you've been saying to me for several months," I replied. "Why don't you just paraphrase it?" In the event, she did not deem paraphrase necessary. At the vestry meeting, she read the letter I'd written on her behalf word for word (sparing us all the delay of source attribution) to the loud approval of her allies, my adversaries. "You really showed him," they crowed, "especially that part about how he never listens to us!" Across the room, I caught our Lord's wink.

AFTER A YEAR the people who were going to leave us had left us — five hundred of them. I missed their faces and the treasurer missed their contributions — but by then nobody much missed their voices, truth be told.

In the meantime Bob Hughes, a friend who teaches Theology at Sewanee,[3] and I had been trying for two years in a row to put together a gathering of "liberal Charismatics," Spirit-baptized people for whom neither voting conservative nor opposing gay people necessarily had the force of a baptismal vow. We called the conference, "Charismatic Spirituality and Modernity." We drafted some governing principles and put out the word.

I remarked to Bob that we could have rented a broom closet to accommodate the conference. We discovered that there are not many "liberal Charismatics" around, and those who are such simply want to be put on your mailing list, to be "kept in the loop."

But those who attended made for a merry gathering, and I found myself more deeply relaxed than I'd been with overtly religious people for many months. We worshiped off and on all day, using the daily offices in the Prayer Book, lodging our discussions in prayer and in the context of the scripture readings. I still recall the aesthetic and emotional thrill I felt bellowing out a song we learned: "Alleluia! The Great Storm Is Over! Lift Up Your Wings and Fly!" It sure fit my life — well, largely.

---

3. St. Luke's School of Theology, University of the South, Sewanee, Tennessee.

It was a lighthearted event, and the banter made its way even into our liturgies. That sprightly tone offered me the freedom to experience the temptation I'm about to report. During a morning liturgy, the reading from Revelation 21 included the words: "I saw no Temple in the City, for its Temple is the Lord God the Almighty and the Lamb." You can guess the sort of wisecrack I was about to make. Everyone there knew how many people were currently predicting my damnation — and the absence of a Temple in heaven looked like a prophetic reference to that devout wish. I felt a twinge of vestigial pain and bitterness as it was read. I decided not to joke about it when I heard: *"Gray, you do that a lot."*

I didn't have to ask, "Do what?" When I feel the onset of emotional pain, I either joke or go abstractly intellectual. Now the Lord was pointing that out unavoidably, judging it — and offering me an alternative. Without words Jesus recalled to me the sense of discovering his presence at the bottom of my terror on Harold's mat. It became clear to me that when I refuse to occupy my pain, I am refusing a meeting with him. He is always waiting within my pain, if I can go into it deeply enough, bravely enough. It has something to do with his cross — and mine. I sat silent for much of the remainder of the liturgy, communing with all the leftover hurts of the previous year or so, trying not to duck any of them. As I did so, Jesus allowed me to feel his deep affection for me — *and* his deep affection for people that in my struggles to stay afloat I'd often been tempted to despise. I was made deeply aware of the *boundlessness* of Jesus's affection, of how it contains room for us all — even adversaries. Yet vast as it is, I realized it contains no room for hiding; at least I wasn't allowed to sneak bitterness into his presence. I eventually told my colleagues what had been taking place. During the rest of the conference several of them remarked, "You're still merry, but something has changed — your playfulness isn't caustic anymore. It's joyous."

THAT'S SOME OF HOW God changed my mind. And it's a story of God staying with me through everything that happened. I knew it was God and not just my imagination because that Presence invariably loved and respected my opponents and antagonists a whole lot more than I did — yet constantly held me safe and precious. (When it's my imagination, my opponents don't come off so well.) In my entire life, God has never told me I was right to the disadvantage of another person — nor allowed me to harbor that notion long in the presence without a gentle upbraiding.

What I've described is an important part of what "reason" means to Episcopalians.

Reason, of course, also means using our understanding, our intellects. And here the church is making heavy weather of it.

Obviously it's my opinion that the considerations I offered in the second chapter about the Bible should be met with more than a snort of derision. Those considerations accord with the most rigorous, disinterested, and faithful thinking about the Bible that can currently be found. I think they show why some of us no longer offer reflex obeisance to appeals to "the plain sense" of scripture; "plain sense" too often goes no deeper into the Bible's complexities than the "common sense" that knows the earth is flat. Yet I expect that few readers had their mind change as a result of reading them. When I've lectured on their basis, the audience participants who already favored gay sacramental equality came out enthusiastic and grateful for the substantiation, while those who were initially opposed were reluctant to meet my gaze. Those considerations produced no mutual engagement, certainly no melding into common community.

That puzzles me. Since prep school I have trusted in good-faith, reasoned discourse to produce a community of understanding. Clearly no such thing has occurred in the country at large as these issues have become a political shuttlecock. That saddens me as an American. So I flee into my identity as a citizen of the kingdom of God seeking humane rationality. Yet even here reasoning about the scriptures in the light of tradition has generated much more heat than light. What is wrong?

In the following discussion, let's reflect on some considerations that could possibly lead to a more fruitful use of rationality on all sides as we wait for God's experiential revelations to grow more widespread.

To begin with, let's clear away any question about whether reason as rigorous discourse has failed us. I want to show that reason has done the best we can realistically expect. Many of us (liberals) in the church think that the primary objections we're used to hearing from opponents of sacramental equality have been squarely met and that our responses to the objections to sacramental equality have not yet been persuasively answered. Because they have been met and linger unanswered, the sticking point has to lie elsewhere.

For now, here is a brief dipstick thrust into these exchanges as they usually go.

1. The Bible says homosexuality is a sin.

Where? The sentence, "Homosexuality is a sin" does not occur in the Bible; neither does the word "homosexuality" — for reasons explained earlier. The Bible does not recognize anything as abstract as "homosexuality." It simply condemns specific actions that don't resemble anything our gay sisters and brothers contemplate.

The Bible condemns several things that we no longer consider sinful. The Bible considers lending money at interest a violation of God's commandment and (in Ezek. 18:13) an abomination. The same with eating shrimp or weasels. On what basis do we privilege one set of prohibitions over others? In no debate in which I've taken part has any opponent answered those questions. All too often their importance goes unrecognized.

2. *Even if the Bible doesn't say homosexuality is a sin in so many words, still you have to admit that heterosexuality is the biblical norm.*

So is being right-handed. And heterosexuality is still a norm that will not be tempered or threatened by homosexuality — any more than my left-handed brother imperils my prevoluntary compliance with the right-handed norm. People who make this point are confusing laws with norms, a confusion that can lead to harsh consequences. I have not yet had an antagonist reply to that — or indeed to acknowledge its force.

3. *The homosexual lifestyle is repellant. Watch the shenanigans at any Gay Pride parade. And how do you justify the bath-houses?*

I won't quarrel with you about the more outlandish behavior and dress the media select to show us whenever there's a parade. And I'm glad San Francisco closed the bathhouses. But it's way past time to quit talking about the "gay lifestyle." If I complained about the "straight lifestyle" and mentioned meat-market bars and swingers' clubs, people would say those aren't typical, that they don't pertain to most of us, although most of us are straight. So I'd ask that we agree to regret elements of the "lifestyle" of unpartnered American human beings rather than hanging it all on gay folk. In offering sacramental equality to homosexual churchgoers the church is taking an alternative position to unpartnered social chaos.

The term "lifestyle" lies at the heart of a serious category confusion. Opponents of sacramental equality tend to use "lifestyle" and "sexual orientation" interchangeably — and they sometimes throw in terms like "sexual preference" and talk about "chosen lifestyle/orientation/preference." In any argument, confusion about the terminology we're using doesn't help the discussion and obscures clear thought. Indeed the assumption that being homoerotically oriented is something a person chooses forms the core of various objections to homosexual persons being recognized as sacramental equals.

Let's repeat what would be obvious if we'd get to know our gay neighbors: people in general do not choose their sexual orientation. I would relish a conversation — or even a debate — with antagonists who were clear about that.

4. *It just isn't natural.*

In fact homogenital behavior is found all over the animal kingdom — ask any zoologist. If you've ever watched your male dog mount another male, the central point of the biblical chapter — that sex was and often still is perceived as an activity for establishing dominance irrespective of the gender of the object — will seem more plausible. Closer to home, supermarket women's magazines breathlessly inform us that only 30 percent of women can achieve satisfaction through conventional missionary-style sexual intercourse. Those magazines recommend measures that many stigmatize as "unnatural." Who wants to tell 70 percent of the women they know, "That's just tough"?

These days we know from linguistic studies that in Paul's day the terms "natural" and "unnatural" referred simply to what was or was not expected. I wonder if we always know what we mean when we use the word. When most of us talk about what's natural or unnatural, the underlying concept of nature is another of those opaque reifications Peter Berger warns us about. Are spectacles natural? We don't come into this world with glasses on. Thomas Aquinas opposed capitalism because it's not natural for an inorganic substance (money) to grow. What do you think about his use of nature? Was he right?

Anne Fausto-Sterling at Brown University has determined that something like 1 percent of hospital births produce infants whose bodies are sexually ambiguous or indeterminate; when surgeons flip a coin and nudge the child in the direction of one sex or the other, they are tragically wrong half the time. What do you want to tell those surgeons, or those children, or those parents, about nature?

All of us know the feeling that some things aren't "natural." Some get it around people with physical disabilities or with disfiguring birthmarks. They may manage to be polite to such people and not to stare, but secretly they wish the disfigured ones hadn't come to the party. In the South white people used to teach their children to avoid the touch of an African American — unless it was the maid bathing them. Erik Erikson at

Harvard coined the term "pseudospeciation" to describe these feelings: protecting ourselves against "otherness" by assigning the "other" to a separate species from ourselves as a squirrel might regard, say, a turtle. Most of us fear the "other" and wish to flee it or drive it off. But is it really wise, humane, or godly to make the pseudospeciation reflex theologically authoritative?

To the present, arguments from "nature" have not carried their own weight.

5. *Homosexuals cannot safely minister to children and young people — so we ought not to ordain them.*

Intensive and widespread research assures us that homosexual orientation is in no way connected with the sexual abuse of children and youth — and the two are far less similar than may at first be apparent. In fact the overwhelming proportion of child molesters are married heterosexuals. Homosexual persons are born; child molesters are made. If you sexually molest a child enough, you will not produce a homosexual adult; you will produce an adult child molester. As urgently important as the safety of our children and the integrity of their sexual boundaries are, the presence or absence of homosexual persons per se simply cannot be shown to be a factor.

Research shows that two groups of people are most likely to molest children. The first is alcoholics. The second is people with rigid belief systems. Some of those rigid belief systems, needless to say, are religious.

6. *Well, the Boy Scouts of America still maintain that homosexual men are not suitable role models for the young.*

And that fact puzzles many of us who otherwise admire the Scouts. It's especially puzzling since the Scouts' own published materials repudiate any connection between homosexuality and pederasty. Are they worried that an admired gay scoutmaster would prompt imitation by the boys he led? If so, they don't know boys very well.[4] When "gay" and "queer" cease to be schoolyard insults, let's start worrying about imitation — though by such a time there may be nothing worrisome left in the issue. Recall again that same-sex orientation is not anything that people choose.

On the other hand there is an important consideration in favor of allowing homosexual adults to be among those who teach and lead the young. For all the validity of the caution that people should not embrace a clear-cut sexual orientation until their late teens, the fact remains that the great majority of homosexual men and women are aware of being "different" from a pretty early age. (Ask their kindergarten teachers.) These children have few positive role models whose examples can offer them some hope for their own futures. Though homosexual kids make up no more than, say, 2 percent of the teen population, 30 percent of teen suicides are despairing youngsters who know they are gay.[5] That is a kind of holocaust, one that we protract by making sure those kids know they have no normal future available to them. Admirable adult

---

4. A Scout executive on his third cocktail recently explained to me that the Scouts *do* know their prime constituency pretty well: 400,000 Boy Scouts come from the Mormon Church. Roman Catholic boys comprise another 350,000. Do the math.

5. Studies on youth suicide consistently find that lesbian and gay youth are two to six times more likely to attempt suicide than other youth and may account for 30 percent of all completed suicides among teens (U.S. Department of Health and Human Services, *Report of the Secretary's Task Force on Youth Suicide*, 101st Cong., 1st sess. [Washington, D.C., 1989]).

gay models are an indispensable part of the solution to that appalling problem.

7. *Homosexuals are acceptable members of the church — but they ought to remain celibate, like alcoholics who join AA and stay dry.*

Why should they remain celibate? For whose sake? For *our* comfort? Do Evangelicals need homosexual believers to agree to remain isolated in order to fund the authority of the conservatives' way of interpreting the Bible? That's a cost Evangelicals need to carry themselves. It's not grown-up to require somebody else to pay that for you at their own emotional and social expense. Celibacy is a gift, a spiritual charism, not a requirement. Under what circumstances would any of us allow someone else to require celibacy of us for the rest of our lives? Why sacrifice the contentment of our homosexual sisters and brothers, few though they be in number, on the altar of our own need to have others subscribe to our way of reading the Bible? Canon Hugh Magers, a staunch-as-oak credentialed Evangelical, reports, "I just can't bring myself to oppose somebody who wants to commit monogamy."

And the comparison with alcoholism is specious. Though recovered sobriety is a lovely miracle of God, nobody ever described alcoholism itself as a means of grace. But discerning Christian people report that some same-sex relationships are quite gracious indeed. In debate when asked to justify their insistence that gay people remain celibate, opponents of same-sex marriage typically (in my experience) blink in incomprehension. This argument may be deeply felt, but it has not so far been well substantiated.

8. *Recently my parish invited an ex-gay speaker in who proved that homosexuals can be healed through prayer, compassionate therapy, and community support. In the light of such presentations, why should we sanction acceptance of practicing homosexual men and women as sacramental equals?*

I've known several such ex-gays personally. They are now ex-ex-gays. They relapse. Many today are with partners they met in ex-gay ministry groups.

Tony Campolo — a noted Evangelical who largely agrees with his coreligionists about most of this — makes a custom of asking the ex-gays he meets the following question: has your reorientation resulted in a change in your *arousal* patterns or in your *fantasy* patterns? He does not report any positive replies.

Both the American Psychiatric and the American Psychological Associations regularly issue warnings concerning the harm incurred in reorientation procedures, whether religious or clinical. Those procedures actually increase the socially imposed self-loathing of homosexual persons. These warnings point out several flaws in the research and treatment models: that they take place within a doctrinaire religious climate; that there are no reliable follow-up or long-term studies to confirm reorientation; that their results are not replicable by others.

That ex-gays continue to dine out on that identity in Evangelical circles testifies to Evangelical willingness to sponsor anything that will shore up their claims to the correctness of their Bible-based idealized construction of things.

If you pray with homosexual Christians you will see God perform any number of miracles. These will often include the expunging of self-loathing, of bitterness toward family and wider society, and relief from previously chaotic patterns of sexual behavior. You will likely not see God reorient many of these seekers to heterosexuality in either their arousal or fantasy patterns. That may eventually prompt you to understand that God does not consider their homosexual orientation a disorder.

Hands-on experience in ministry among gay men and women complete with follow-up will eventually put this argument to rest.

9. *Marriage is for conceiving, bearing, and rearing children. Homosexuals cannot have children, and so they should not marry.*

The bearing and raising of children is one of several important parts of marriage, but again this statement confuses a norm with a law. If producing children were a requirement of marriage, we would not permit our widowed mothers to remarry, right? Read the Bible. Abraham did not divorce Sarah because of her barrenness. Nowhere in the Christian scriptures is childbearing offered as the purpose of marriage — not in any speech of our Lord's, not in any letter of Paul's. Judaism got clear about that point two thousand years ago; it's our turn.

In fact there are two important reasons for marriage that take priority over childbearing. The first is the domestication of males — seriously. The second is the socially urgent matter of assuring that as many of us possible have a primary caregiver nearby. The latter is no small consideration in this day when the true face of Compassionate Conservatism is emerging.

146

*10. I guess I could go along with some sort of domestic partnership
arrangement and maybe even a blessing of their "union." But
why do you have to insist that it's "marriage"?*

Many of us insist on recognizing same-sex unions as marriage
for several reasons. It will hold gay unions accountable to the
same disciplines the rest of us try to live by — like fidelity
and permanence. Phrased positively it shelters us all under the
same moral canopy. It compels all of us to recognize that marriage is not primarily constituted by its externals — a man and
a woman — but by the relationship itself: faithful, truthful,
mutual, and permanent. Marriage can now be seen as the intersection of God's grace and human loyalty and courage, rather
than simply the coalescence of genital concavities and convexi-
ties. It will reinforce and shore up the marital institution itself
that today is sinking toward minority status.

Why not take this occasion, when there is at least a chance of
deepening our understanding of the essential substance of marriage — a sacramental relationship undergirded by God — to do
a much better job than ever to vet *all* applicants for the marriage
sacrament? Marriage, like Holy Orders, is a vocation from God
that the congregation is supposed to discern and ratify. Could
we work together to put real teeth into that responsibility?

11. The church is once again giving in to the world.

"Halleluiah!" say I. It's not pleasant for any of us to admit that
the primary advances in social justice and well-being of the last
century or so have resulted from social forces apart from the
church's witness. The unions made the market work for them
and produced an era of economic well-being for all — twice, on
either side of the Depression. It was merchants who integrated

the South as they realized that black money spends as well as white. It has been the market that insists that if women are allowed responsibility in a corporation, that company makes more money than its sexist competitors. The same thing is happening today with domestic partnership policies. Do you think the Disney Corporation would have risked the ire of the Southern Baptist Convention if it thought it could flourish without its gay employees? The evidence points to the conclusion that the Holy Spirit currently finds the world of more service than the church in nudging society toward the kingdom. In effect, it is rarely enough to stigmatize the origin of a movement as "worldly" in order to oppose it theologically or spiritually.

There are few racists on either side of the pro/anti-gay divide. Neither are there many anti-feminine bigots on either side. And as much as we all love the language of the 1928 Prayer Book, we have reluctantly forfeited it in order to offer the grace of liturgical worship to people who are marginalized by that language. In all of those matters, the church was thought by some to give in. Which of them do we regret?

Tradition, as I discussed in the previous chapter, tends to support and maintain the status quo, and we have learned over the centuries that the status quo is often hostile to social justice and civil rights. The status quo is not a reliable theological litmus test.

12. *Homosexual "marriage" will alter marriage as we know it in both definition and practice.*

This is the most frustrating point that regularly gets raised in our debates. The obvious rejoinder is to ask, "How?" How do Adam and Steve calling themselves a married couple alter or exercise any detectable impact whatsoever on my marriage to Jean? In countless conversations and in three nationally publicized debates I have asked that question — on stage and privately. I have never yet heard it answered, even implausibly. Instead my interlocutors have simply repeated the claim with evident self-approval as though the question demanded no answer — sometimes three times running. This assertion seems autistically tautological and circular.

At this juncture, permit a lengthy parenthesis on the reciprocal impacts between homosexuality and marriage.

Even if that anti-gay claim is, on its face, irrational, still no one can deny that it is utterly serious. It deserves a closer look.

The relation between men and women itself is undergoing seismic change today in ways that affect us all and generate great anxiety. Since 1960, the rate of heterosexual couples cohabiting without marriage has multiplied tenfold. At the same time fewer young people have marriage in view. Without question those developments are altering "marriage as we know it." Equally beyond question is the fact that homosexual persons have had no influence on that shift whatever. For most of that period, homosexuality has simply not been on our radar screens. That in itself might answer the charge against gay marriage as a social change factor.

But let's go further. Let's briefly examine the history of marriage using an economic model.

Think of service/comfort/pleasure as a commodity that "women" produce for "men" to consume.[6] Look at marital history through that lens. In the ancient world down to

---

6. Let's maintain the understanding of gender construction that we explored in chapter 2: man = powerful human being, woman = (relatively) powerless human being.

very recent centuries, men owned the means of production — women. Men could buy, sell, and collect women. (Think of mail-order brides, dowries, polygamy, or harems.) Prostitutes might retail themselves, but the pimp lurked around the corner.

Over the course of many centuries, parts of Western culture evolved to the point where finally, in the twentieth century, *women* owned the means of production — their own bodies. A woman could no longer legally be bought, sold, or owned. Their chastity — always an important ancillary commodity in cultures where men worry about the legitimacy of their progeny — remained fungible, something a woman could "sell" to a man in exchange for a lifetime of sharing his income. Sociologists call this institution "companionate marriage."

The latter sexual economy was largely governed by women, as was the Victorian economy that preceded it. Women "saved themselves for marriage." Cliques of high school girls determined "how much the boys could have" on first, second, and third dates. The culture, often represented by the church, functioned something like the Federal Reserve Bank, helping women maintain the value of the sexual currency, punishing inflationary behavior (sex for free).

Since World War II, when women entered the salaried work force in massive numbers, women have been moving closer to financial autonomy — reducing the pressure for self-indenture to men. With the advent of the Pill, women were finally men's sexual peers: that is, women could participate in sex without fear of pregnancy — just like men. That in turn introduced a male-terrifying novelty: sexual comfort is no longer something women produce for men; it is now something women expect men to produce for *them* as well.

The latter recent developments scare many of us — this writer included. We do not yet know how human interpersonal sexual relations will settle out and self-institutionalize. We are in a period of chaos whether we like it or not.[7]

If the church could maintain a voice in the current discussion, that could well be a very good thing. The church has a revolutionary message, bequeathed to us both by our Lord and St. Paul: the renunciation of dominance in all relations. Surely that includes seductiveness and manipulation. If our culture could be nudged in that direction, we might indeed be happy with the outcome.

But for the church to squander what little attention we can attract by insisting that the culture return to a companionate-marriage sexual economy is equivalent to aged economists insisting that the United States restore the gold standard. As the old James Russell Lowell hymn taught us, "They must upward, still, and onward, who would keep abreast of Truth."

Three final observations. First, the church's traditional role as supervisor of the sexual currency is nearly over — and that scares us. That may account for the church's relentless preoccupation with sex: abortion, birth control, divorce, and homosexuality. Where is the church's voice on issues much more central to the heart of God as reflected in the scriptures, issues such as war and peace, economic justice, and the beauty of the Earth? Most Americans, including most Christians, think religion is mostly about sexual repression.

---

7. Recall, though, that chaos is best understood as that phase in an ongoing process in which we are not yet able to discern a pattern; but the pattern eventually emerges, often more complex than the pattern it displaced.

Second, the changes in marriage rates, cohabitation, and sexual reciprocity have indeed affected "marriage as we know it." And the "homosexual lifestyle" — made necessary by the culture's refusal to recognize their relationships — has indeed served as the emblem of what we fear. I think that's what people mean when they say that homosexuality harms marriage. That's a mistaken connection, of course. But the heterosexuals who adopted the license that previously homosexuals modeled (though there's no evidence that they learned it from homosexuals) have indeed indubitably harmed "marriage as we know it."

Third, the wish of at least some homosexual Christians to have their pairings solemnized and made permanent within the sacrament of Holy Matrimony is a *conservative* development. What we have in this small community is a group of men and women who have withdrawn voluntarily from the chaotic meat-market Friday night scene in order to construct a permanent relationship based on mutual love. These men and women are pioneers; they are the first to emerge from the chaos that so properly scares us. We need their voices. We need their courage, their wit, their inventiveness. We need their prayers.

If we're *really* serious about maintaining the American family, then let's join hands in opposing the actual forces that are doing families the most damage. Let's oppose advertising campaigns that harness our (marital) sexual dissatisfactions to sell us commodities we neither need nor can afford, offering us the televised illusion of polygamy. Let's oppose the efforts of the last few administrations to break the dwindling power of trade unions under the guise of free trade, unions being the only voices in our civilization interested in an economy that pays a full family wage to a single worker. Let's meet our full tax obligation — the lowest in the developed world, for God's sake — and insist that the proceeds go to decent schools for everyone, affordable housing and health care for all of us, and for social services to buffer vulnerable families against catastrophe.

THAT LIST OF OBJECTIONS is fairly typical of what comes up in debates at all levels in the church, from the Primates' meetings with the Archbishop of Canterbury down to a parish undercroft. The replies are typical of what we liberals usually respond with.

Often the objections don't rise to that level. Recently I was on a panel at a local university with a seminary professor who knit his brow and expressed "profound doubts" about homosexuality and confessed that he harbored "grave reservations" — as though his personal unsubstantiated doubts and reservations were authoritative in themselves. He proceeded to assert that gay men and women were either mistaken or deceptive in their understanding of their own lives. I found myself wondering if such arrogance were the fruit of years wielding a red pencil over hapless students. The audience was remarkably polite in view of their frustrated expectation of hearing reason from a credentialed academic.

So we need to seek additional considerations if we are to understand why our reasoning so far has not brought us closer to each other. And a prime candidate for consideration is human development. A person's view on the matter of sacramental equality for gay and lesbian Christians is a good predictor of his or her position on any number of maturity scales. Though it is in terrible taste to bring that up, I believe we cannot understand our current conversational gridlock until we confront that truth.

A couple of initial anecdotes may illustrate the pertinence of taking developmental stages into account when we find ourselves in disagreement with others.

During the period that my parish was convulsing over the issue we're discussing, a woman brought me a letter from her daughter, a Religion major in an out-of-state university. I'll never forget the light that went on as she read me the following passage: "I guess I'm really not surprised to read about the strong reaction against Gray and his position on homosexuality. To people at stage four, people at stage five or above must always appear evil." At the time I'd not yet read James Fowler's *Stages of Faith*, yet I sensed at once what she meant.

Over the next few years as I got reacquainted with Abraham Maslow's work, as I read Fowler, Brian Hall, Ken Wilber, and any number of others, it became clear to me that a person's declared position on a subject is the minimum of what you need to know when entering a discussion or debate with them. You will shortly benefit from some sense of how grown-up they are. Here's another anecdote:

In the late 1950s my seminary advisor, Dr. Jack Beckwith, was the rector of a conservative church in Charleston, South Carolina. His vestry was seeking a way to force his resignation owing to his heroically liberal outlook on racial integration. In the nick of time Virginia Seminary pulled him out of the fracas by calling him to their faculty.

At his final vestry meeting, Jack looked around the room with amusement and said, "I'm told that you gentlemen have already formed a committee to seek my replacement — and that you seek a rector whose views on race differ from mine."

No reply — just looks of sullen abashment.

Jack went on, "I have just one thing to say to you about that: if you succeed in finding such a man, his views on race are the only thing about him that'll suit you!"

So it proved. Why? Because, as Jack well knew, racism is not a characteristic of mature human beings — and congregations prefer mature clergy to immature.

Many a parish has made a similar discovery in rector searches. It's so easy to assume that the most important thing about a candidate is what she says she believes this year. Of more importance, however, is her personal maturity — especially her capacity for empathy.

So let's consider this important matter of development.

REASON IS THE MOST VEXING of the three vectors we are considering because we repeatedly experience our wheels spinning in conversation with those who disagree. Considerations that strike us as well founded, that we know to be well substantiated, so often get no traction in our discussions. We sometimes have the feeling that we do not inhabit the same cognitive universe with those we're facing — even though we too love the Lord our God with all our hearts, souls, minds, and strength as do they. The same can probably be said for those on the other side of the debate — certainly they exhibit the sense of facing aliens. I hope it's safe to assume everyone wants to do the right thing and believes that they know what the right thing is. Yet both sides know that's not enough.

The discussions we've had for thirty years have changed few minds either way, and most of us have proved impervious to the "drift toward the middle." At no point has liberal reasoning or conservative truth-proclamation tempted the interlocutors to agreement. Even though I consider everything I've written so far as the very model of rationality, the few conservative readers who have made it this far probably remain unmoved.

Why? Because I have been arguing out of the context of my own cognitive universe, describing how the world appears to me from my current developmental level. To do better it's necessary to put the matter of personal development onto the table — my own and that of my antagonists. This consideration needs more widespread attention on both sides of the debate. That it has not played much of a role so far in our conversations in the church likely owes to the wish of many not to commit a breach of good manners. But it's relevant enough that the church can no longer delay finding some way to manage it.

The fact is that those who favor and those who oppose sacramental equality for gay and lesbian Christians do inhabit different cognitive universes — even if we inhabit the same families, congregations, and cultural strata. Our cognitive universes are constructed by what we want and what we fear. Those two elements shift to different objects over time. As our lives proceed, the various circumstances we encounter alter, expand, and shrink our desires and fears.

A few semesters in a college fraternity may eventually persuade us that the pleasures of binge drinking and throwing up all over our dates have been somewhat overrated. By God's grace and the charm of various teachers we may also grow into a suspicion that the pleasures of learning, of reading the metaphysical poets, of mastering calculus, of learning the thought forms of a previously unfamiliar language, had been somewhat underrated. Before we were married, our worst fear was personal extinction; once we were married our worst fear was our spouse's extinction; once we became parents, our worst fear was of harm to our children. Unless something happens to us to get us stuck, our worldview will slowly expand. Simply put, our fears and longings will shift to different objects. However, if you scare us badly enough our wants (e.g., world peace) will quickly revert to a previous level (get me out of here!).

Those shifts upward and downward were studied by some of the most fertile minds of the twentieth century.

Those of us educated in the sixties can still recall the thrill of first reading Abraham Maslow and exploring his "hierarchy of needs."[8] That schema is so familiar as to need little explanation here. Maslow sensibly explained that if you can't get your breath, the fact that you're thirsty can wait. If you're out of water, your hunger can wait. When you have enough air, water, and food, you can worry about how cold or hot it is. Once you know that you can control your body temperature, you can pay attention to the people around you — like whether or not you can trust them. If you find you can trust them at least to some extent, you can afford to worry about whether or not they like you. Then you can decide whether or not you like them. Then you can afford to imagine what you could create as a community of friends. Your hopes and fears grow broader; they ascend to a sense of relatedness with and responsibility for the very cosmos.

Now let's consider what happens under stress. If something blocks your air hose when you're diving, you descend Maslow's hierarchy of needs abruptly. Under stress we regress to previous levels.

---

8. Abraham Maslow, *Toward a Psychology of Being* (New York: Van Nostrand, 1962).

Back when Episcopal clergy routinely received training in the dynamics of groups we learned that when a group first comes together, its members are worried about "inclusion" issues: Do I want to be a member? Is membership safe or desirable? If enough of us remain in the fledgling group, we move to issues of "control": Who has conversational right-of-way in here? How much power do I have? If the members find those questions clarified sufficiently to hang in with the group, issues of "affection" will prevail: Shall I risk loving or trusting these people? How close are we going to get?

So far, so good. But if a fight breaks out or some external stress hits an affection-preoccupied group, it will revert back to control anxiety: Who's in charge? Do I have enough power in here? The group may even get blasted back into inclusion anxiety: Do I still want to belong to this group?

Something like that happens to individuals. In discussions with folks I disagree with, as I get more and more worked up over the stiff opposition to my convictions about gay Episcopalians, it may not escape your notice that I sound more and more like an aggrieved and querulous teenager. That is, of course, a regression from the normally serene, almost mystical tranquility for which I am so widely esteemed.

It can happen to any of us at any time.[9]

---

9. The philosopher-mathematician Bertrand Russell was immersed in a romantic tryst in a London hotel during the Blitz when a bomb exploded nearby. He sprang from the bed, ripped the sheet from it that had been covering his erstwhile lover, wrapped it about himself as a sort of toga, and made to bolt from the room. "What about me?" shrieked his companion. He retained the presence of mind to reply, "My dear, perfect fear casteth out love!"

I've couched this discussion in terms of Maslow's magisterial work with which we're all familiar. That work no longer protrudes in isolation. Developmental themes have been fruitfully refined by researchers like Erik Erikson, Lawrence Kohlberg, James Fowler, and any number of others. One researcher, Brian P. Hall, has mapped the course of a typical individual's progress in value formation, defining four phases representing four successive worldviews, each of which contains two stages.[10]

Hall reports that we begin with a worldview in which the world is apprehended as *a threatening mystery over which we have no control* (phase I).

We may then move to a worldview in which the world is *a problem with which we must cope* (phase II).

If we manage to move out of that phase, there is a chance that our worldview will change to one in which the world is *a project in which we participate* (phase III).

Eventually in Hall's final phase we may apprehend the world as a mystery again, this time *a sacred mystery for which we must care* (phase IV).

In phase I, in which the world is a terrifying mystery, there are two stages: *safety* — the physical safety of my body (1) and *security* — my ability to trust my physical and social environment to meet my needs (2). In phase II, in which the world is a problem we must cope with, the two stages are *family* — knowing I belong to a loyal small community (3) and *institution* — belonging to a reliable larger society (4). Phase III, in which the world is a project inviting participation, the stages are *vocation* — doing work that has value (5) and *new order* — seeing my work matter beyond my own frame of reference (6). Finally in

---

10. Brian P. Hall, *The Genesis Effect* (New York: Paulist Press, 1986).

phase IV, in which the world is a mystery to be cherished, the stages are *wisdom* — pulling it all together within my own heart (7) and *world order* — offering my heart to the cosmos (8).

The precision of Hall's understanding and development of these phases and stages is such that I blush to summarize them so casually — and the supplied examples are my own simplifications. I summarize nevertheless in order to be able to introduce an urgent point that Hall offers people caught in contretemps such as ours in the church. Hall's research shows that attempts at communication between people who are two or more *stages* (not phases) removed from each other can at best hope for no more than a 20 percent mesh.

Please pause to weigh that.

I recall once conversing with an energetic psychologist at a conference at which I felt nervous and out of my depth. In retrospect, in my anxious condition I was at about phase I stage 2. He was at least at phase III stage 5. He got more and more invasive (as I experienced it) in his questions about me and my work with groups of undergraduates, and at one point he ventured, "I'd enjoy working with you." The conversation plummeted steeply downhill from there. It only occurred to me days later he'd been saying, "I'd like to collaborate with you on some projects." A compliment, in effect. But I'd understood him to mean, "You need for me to work *on* you as a therapist." The latter was probably true.

In more simplistic terms, if my hopes and fears are perceptively out of sync with yours, we miss four-fifths of each other's meanings. Does that feel familiar? Does that help us grasp why we have enjoyed so little mutual engagement in all our "dialogues," why our proclamations have fallen on deaf ears? Does

that help us see why we have enriched each other's understandings — let alone each other's very lives — so little in the thirty
years or so that we have been working on the issue before us?

The fact that in any roomful of people several developmental
stages are likely present makes it important that we be clear
about some implications of these differences.

First, until we achieve a kind of spiritual breakthrough into
sensing how God delights in people who don't immediately
delight us, we will tend to despise and scorn anyone on a different developmental level. As my undergraduate friend and
supporter knew, we fear and resent people who are developmentally above and beyond us. Remember the phrase, "Effete
intellectual snobs"? Remember who coined it?[11]

Second, extremely intelligent or clever people are not necessarily very evolved. Intelligence or cleverness are not the same
as maturity. We all know of surgeons who throw tantrums in
the operating room.

Third, the further we progress in emotional/values/spiritual
development, the less prone we'll be to self-approval, the less
we'll preen ourselves with our opinions.

That latter point supplies a clue to the fifth thing to keep
in mind about development: progress in personal development can be measured by the extent to which we relinquish
egocentricity.

Let's dwell on the latter consideration.

Any number of researchers on human development report
that advancement from stage to stage is best understood and

---

11. It was Spiro Agnew, the disgraced vice president, later thrown to the
wolves to forestall Watergate.

undertaken as growth away from egocentricity. By egocentricity, researchers mean to describe an actual inability rather than a moral failing, the inability to abstract how reality must appear to another person not ourselves. The challenge past egocentricity is to learn to "see from the other side," as Robert Greenleaf used to phrase it. Considering — really straining to consider — that reality looks and feels differently to another person is a gentling exercise. And it is abetted as we each discover, forgive, and — yes — *cherish* the other person's level of consciousness within ourselves, past as well as present.

Talk of egocentricity sounds harsh. Before we judge "egocentric" people harshly, let's each put ourselves into the position of, say, a parent whose teenage son has just come out of the closet to the family. Abruptly the wave function of rich possibilities in the future — of a future daughter-in-law, of grandchildren — has collapsed. None of that is going to happen. If it's a daughter who comes out, there will no wedding plans that so bond brides and their mothers, no proud dad walking his daughter down the aisle. That's a shock to the whole system. As we know, shocks induce regression. The teen's parents will predictably regress to the developmental position of strict traditional biblical morality — and under some circumstances will be tempted to reenter the previous developmental zone of order-through-violence.

The brain is a conservative organ and changes its view of things quite slowly. It will be quite a while before we can reasonably expect either parent to endeavor to see things from the standpoint of the gay youngster, to welcome their various partners, to resume their erstwhile social pride in their offspring. These people are not being "selfish"; under those circumstances few of us could do better.

A husband whose wife takes a deep breath one evening and explains that she has come to realize that she is lesbian will not rush to see things from the perspective of the wife he loves. He will bellow about her selfishness and shout about the laws of God and man until he's blue in the face — even if by day he edits a radical ecological journal. The jolt of his collapsing future requires management. He must regress.

That is not a matter of the presence or the absence of virtue. It is a simply a description of human neurological wiring. Some people indeed snap back to awareness of the other person fairly quickly, but they do so with seismic internal effort.

Conservative egocentricity is never so coarse as, say, taking the biggest piece of cake. Rather it is the preconscious preference of one's own equanimity, one's own inner peace, to considering what the inner reality of another person might look and feel like. In some circumstances that preference is a requirement for survival. It was not for nothing that in the Greek text of John 15:13 Jesus actually said, "No one has greater love than this, to lay down one's *psyche* (life) for one's friends." Our reaction to such announcements as I've described skirts the near proximity of madness.

That reaction is not under patent to conservatives.[12] It's simply that conservatives tend to enshrine that reaction in policy, confusing it with doctrine.

Now the liberal conversational agenda appears to draw more heavily on Hall's upper phases and stages. But original sin remains widespread and can be detected at any point on the developmental spectrum. Liberal egocentricity takes the form

---

12. Why stigmatize conservatives at all by locating them lower on the developmental food chain? Because Hall's first two phases look more like

of preferring what we are today to what we were. In refusing to claim and find a place for our own earlier developmental levels whose traits, after all, never fully fade, and in despising those traits in others, we contribute to the autoimmune disease that will always afflict any society that does not select emotionally and spiritually mature leadership. Liberal impatience with the parents of gay kids who revert to rigid religiosity amounts to a refusal to recognize one's own darkness and vulnerability.

Once we take the unavoidable process of development into account, reason itself points the way through our current heated discussion about sacramental equality — and that way emerges as *spiritual.*

Earlier I mentioned that both sides have withheld themselves from the risky venture of exploratory prayer, an essential

---

the conservative conversational agenda than otherwise, for one thing. For another reason, I have in front of me a case study entitled "Political Conservatism as Motivated Social Cognition," conducted by Professors John I. Jost of Stanford, Jack Glaser and Frank J. Sulloway of UC at Berkeley, and Arie W. Kluglanski of the University of Maryland at College Park. A glance at its abstract will convey the sense: "Analyzing political conservatism as motivated social cognition integrates theories of personality (authoritarianism, dogmatism-intolerance of ambiguity), epistemic and existential needs (for closure, regulatory focus, terror management), and ideological rationalization (social dominance, system justification). A meta-analysis (88 samples, 12 countries, 22,818 cases) confirms that several psychological variables predict political conservatism: death anxiety (weighed mean $r = .50$); system instability (.47); dogmatism-intolerance of ambiguity (.34); openness to experience (-.32); uncertainty tolerance (-.27); need for order, structure, and closure (.26); integrative complexity (-.20); fear of threat and loss (.18); and self-esteem (-.09). The core ideology of conservatism stresses resistance to change and justification of inequality and is motivated by needs that vary situationally and dispositionally to manage uncertainty and threat." They were studying political conservatism, not social conservatism, so it should be applied to this discussion with caution.

element in reason as Hooker apprehended it. Both sides, to be sure, pray petitions like, "Send confusion to our enemies," or, "O God, change their minds"; or, "Prosper our cause," the *Gott Mit Uns* sort of prayer. But that's not *exploratory* prayer. Exploratory prayer asks and expects God to expand our cramped view of things and to change our hearts — on God's own terms rather than our own.

At least two spiritual operations are central to exploratory prayer.

The first is *repentance* — as Jesus meant it.

As anyone who listens to gospel sermons surely knows, *metanoia* is more than an exercise in guilt. It's interesting that the first three gospels show Jesus preaching *metanoia* directly following his emergence from his wilderness temptations. In the wilderness, as Mark tells us (Mark 1:12–13), Jesus knew the Holy Spirit was driving the process; he was removed from his normal comforts and palliatives; he faced into unmitigated evil; he confronted animal nature in himself as well as his surroundings; and he discovered the strengthening encouragement of the very angels of God. The whole experience turned him inside out. When he came out of the wilderness everything looked different. *Jesus* had repented — that is, he had changed his mind about everything he thought he'd known previously. He was for the first time prepared to follow his calling. Is it too much to assume that Jesus requires that of each of us today — and has offered us this controversy as a suitable occasion?

It ought to be clear from this discussion that if any conservative Evangelical is wondering what she ought to repent of, I have a little list ready. Specifically our common life would improve measurably if conservative Evangelicals would repent to the extent of embracing cognitive self-doubt. Their co-religionist Peter Berger could point the way with his discussions of reification, of alienation, of the social construction of reality. It's natural for each of us to assume that our minds with their present furnishings are a stable platform from which we can view the world accurately. But to consider that it could be otherwise, that our grasp of things may be somewhat conditioned, hence conditional, is the beginning of wisdom.

Less evident (in this discussion, at least) is the list of mind changes (we) liberals have before us. Were we to change our minds so as to become recognizably akin to conservative Evangelicals, we might do well to snuggle up to the real world wherein they earnestly strive to live. We might confess our liberal refusal to admit that hierarchies of value and competence exist all over the place: that is, not all opinions are equal, and nobody believes we mean it when we say, "There are no wrong answers." When we deny that people are responsible for their own choices and insist that the outside environment is the culprit, nobody believes us. Conservatives have little reason to think we believe original sin is evenly distributed. They detect the patronizing didactic tone beneath our insistences. We may eschew distinctions between good and bad and various classes of people, but in so doing we come off as elitist.

Differently put, dogmatic liberals tend to be so proud no longer to be religiously or culturally dogmatic that we forget that there is little to choose between dogmatisms. The resolution to the culture wars does not lie in everyone turning liberal. It lies in a lot of traditionally religious people, a lot of pragmatic hard-chargers, and a lot of social idealists exploring ways of being together that actively seek the contribution of each. We need to get on with it. When we do, we will feel safer for our religiously traditional colleagues to fraternize with — and less contemptible to our practical, what's-all-the-fuss colleagues.

Our liberal epistemological mistakes are more than the simple misreading of reality's data. They result from our refusal to heed our own internal data. We mostly have not acknowledged, claimed, forgiven, and learned to cherish those vestigial elements in each of our depths that remain forever survival-preoccupied, or clannish, or force-reliant, or dogmatic, or impatient with the impalpable. Trendy as it must sound, I actually experience my tolerance and affection for opponents growing to the extent that I succeed in embracing my own "inner Republican." My ongoing refusal to do so more frequently and deeply is a matter of *metanoia*.

The second spiritual operation is *forgiveness*. Jesus began teaching people to forgive each other at about the same time as or only shortly after he taught repentance. Much has been said and written about forgiveness. But for the present let's simply understand it as the acceptance of other persons exactly as they are, giving them the gift of sparing them the deserved consequences of whatever hurtful actions they have directed toward us. To forgive another person is to go to our private cross on that person's behalf.

When we forgive ourselves, the result is humility — humility as Kierkegaard understood it: perfect self-acceptance. In developmental terms, that requires that I recognize and make space for all my primitive propensities even though I choose to keep some of that material in check. If we can achieve sufficient humility, forgiving others is measurably less wrenching.

All of that is strenuous, herniating work. Until we reach a state where we can actively sense how God values people we disapprove of and disagree with, forgiveness will always be a deliberate effort, the sort of thing we briefly explore and enjoy at retreats and then promptly abandon once we're back home. Only safely in God's presence where we can sense God's delight in those we fear does forgiveness become a reflex habit. In fact, the fastest way I know to pick people out of a crowd who live in God's presence is to identify people who hold no grudges.

Yet these efforts at repentance, forgiveness, and the acquisition of humility promise a payoff for all the wrenching effort required. The abandonment of egocentricity is the fastest path to values maturity: the level of internal development in which we no longer fear or despise the developmentally previous coils of consciousness in ourselves or others. We might be able to hear each other's fears and wishes clearly and allow them to resonate within ourselves, to collaborate with each other in the pursuit of common values.

Our spontaneous efforts at this stage will seek to form communities that, like God's own house, contain many dwellings, mansions enough for all. And as we work at loving people whom God loves we may be rewarded with the sense that what we do reverberates through a stratum of the cosmos we had previously never perceived directly, the stratum within which the great cloud of witnesses so apparent to the writer of the Letter to the Hebrews (12:1) takes up our efforts into their own.

ONCE WHEN GOD spoke to us directly about "reason" (at least in the King James Version), it was in the context of being already forgiven:

> Come now, let us argue it out (KJV: "reason together")
>   says the LORD:
> though your sins are like scarlet,
>   they shall be like snow;

> though they are red like crimson,
> they shall become like wool. (Isa. 1:18)

The fact that we are making any headway at all in the discussions about sacramental equality offers us hope that God's invitation is still open — on the same gracious terms.

Epilogue

The human heart can go the lengths of God.
Dark and cold we may be, but this
Is no winter now. The frozen misery
of centuries breaks, cracks, begins to move;

The thunder is the thunder of the floes,
The thaw, the flood, the upstart Spring.
Thank God our Time is now when wrong
Comes up to face us everywhere,

Never leave us till we take
The longest stride of soul men ever took.
Affairs are now soul size.
The enterprise
Is exploration into God.
Where are you making for? It takes
So many thousand years to wake
But will you wake for pity's sake?

— CHRISTOPHER FRY,
A Sleep of Prisoners

In the Fourth Gospel our Lord delivers an intimate address to those to whom he was closest, those who had been with him from the beginning. At one point he said something perfectly terrifying: "I still have many things to say to you, but you cannot bear them now" (John 16:12).

He went on to promise them the Spirit of Truth who will remain among us forever, one whose office is to reveal those concealed matters to us bit by bit, always slightly in advance of our readiness to receive them.

The Jerusalem disciples did not initially want to hear anything favorable about Cornelius and his household from Peter or anyone else. The church of Constantine's day did not want to be served by clergy and bishops who had fled and abandoned them in persecution — and some, the Donatists, refused for several centuries. We think of the Protestant Reformation as the great period when Christians realized the authority of the single believer alone with his (usually not her) Bible, yet most Protestants were as chary of the resulting "anarchy" as were the popes and cardinals. Only the Pietists thought that was a good idea — and at great cost. Centuries later it remained costly to recognize that God favors neither slavery nor racial discrimination — the cost being that of confronting one's own past smug bigotry *sub specie aeternitatis*.

In each of those matters and in many thousands of others, public and private, the Spirit has faced the same task with Jesus's people: to introduce gently the understanding that *the voice of my private sensibilities is not the voice of God*. God's voice simply does not sound to empower me to the harm of others. Ever. Righteous indignation is simply anger. It evaporates in God's actual presence, which may furnish a clue as to its origin. When I love the sinner but hate the sin, pretty soon I hate both.

I think the Spirit is addressing the church on the matter of sacramental equality for homosexual members. I think this betokens good news for us at each of the levels we have considered.

The Spirit agrees with all of us who treasure the Bible as a — perhaps the — primary source of divine revelation. To that effect, the Spirit is driving us back to our Bibles on this matter.

The result for many of us will be a detachment from the canonical interpretations with which we had shielded ourselves from God's fresh voice.

The Spirit of Jesus Christ would have us grasp the real tradition of marriage. The tradition is not primarily something external, like its customary male/female sexual constituency. Rather the essence of marriage is the courage and generosity with which two persons commit to each other in truthfulness, mutuality, fidelity, and the expectation of permanence. The tradition started, as we saw, in Genesis 2 in which Adam *chose*. We had become altogether too complacent about marriage, the mounting divorce rate notwithstanding. But the "Gay Challenge" both compels a much needed re-embrace of the authentic deep tradition of marriage and offers fresh sisters and brothers who, by dint of having been previously excluded, prize "traditional marriage" even more than many of the already married. This is not a curse or a threat; it is Christ's restorative gift to all of us.

The Spirit has re-presented to the Episcopal Church what the authentic church tradition has always been: so to love one another as Christ has loved us that we lay down our lives for each other, contemplating denominational extinction if need be in service of God's truth. Heretofore we'd been pretty faithful to one of Jesus's commandments at the Last Supper — the part about, "Do this for the remembrance of me." God knows, we've paid attention to that one. Now Jesus is re-presenting us with the New Commandment to love each other sacrificially. To shrink from that divine challenge is neither faithful nor orthodox, regardless of who says it is.

And, in our very frustrations over the impotence of what we'd understood as reason to bring forth a common mind in the church about our gay and lesbian brothers and sisters, we are being compelled to reclaim that most central element of reasoning that is precisely ... spiritual. Our contempt and suspicion of one another pose us a clear divine command both to love "enemies" and embrace the enemy within ourselves. We ourselves are confronted by the old Frenchman who, standing in the burnt ruins of his village and facing starvation, could observe, "The final sadness is that we're not saints."

You and I are not saints either. That's terribly sad. It's also something that the Spirit knows how to fix — if allowed to.

When I feel no sympathy or mutual understanding for someone with whom I'm arguing, I am not necessarily being challenged to be more right or correct than they. Jesus nowhere commanded us to be correct or unmistaken. The Holy Spirit is introducing an alternative to us: to sit at table with one another until conviviality produces a new community where partisanship had previously estranged us from each other. Like many of our Lord's commands, that's considerably more charming that what usually occurs to us on our own. God's gift to us takes the form of new friends and colleagues to treasure.

Don't despair or allow yourself to get embittered, dearly beloved.

This is God's doing.